Contents

Acknowledgments   vii
Preface   ix

1. Stop and Think   1
2. The Ferrari: A Wake-Up Call   11
3. Digestion Made Simple   19
4. Habit Number One: Don't Smoke   43
5. Habit Number Two: Don't Drink Alcohol   49
6. Habit Number Three: Don't Take Drugs   53
7. Habit Number Four: Exercise   59
8. Habit Number Five: Eat Right   65
9. Habit Number Six: Clean Your Mind   91
10. Habit Number Seven: Cleanse Your Body   97
11. Bring the Whole Family Along   103

Notes   107
Index   111
About the Author   116

Habits of
Healthy Living

Andrew Tutino

Vitasta
Let Knowledge Spread

Times
Group
Books

The information contained in this book is based upon the research, and personal and professional experiences of the author. It is not intended as a substitute for consulting with your physician or other healthcare provider. Any attempt to diagnose and treat an illness should be done under the direction of a healthcare professional. The publisher does not advocate the use of any particular healthcare protocol but believes the information in this book should be available to the public.

The publisher and author are not responsible for any adverse effects or consequences resulting from the use of the suggestions, preparations, or procedures discussed in this book. Should the reader have any questions concerning the appropriateness of any procedures or preparation mentioned, the author and the publisher strongly suggest consulting a professional healthcare advisor.

Published in 2012 by
Vitasta Publishing Pvt. Ltd.
2/15, Ansari Road, Daryaganj,
New Delhi - 110 002
info@vitastapublishing.com

6 13

ISBN 978-93-80828-25-1
© Andrew Tutino

First Published as Stop and Think: The seven habits of healthy living by Basic Health Publications, Inc., USA
Laguna Beach, CA 92651, USA

Cover Design and Layout by Vitasta Publishing Pvt. Ltd.
Printed by Vits,Press, New Delhi

Marketed and Distributed exclusively in India & Sub-Continent by:

Times Group Books
(A division of Bennett, Coleman and Company Limited)
Times Annexe, Express Building
9-10 Bahadur Shah Zafar Marg, New Delhi-110 002

*I dedicate this book
to my dad, in loving memory:*

Antonino Tutino

*He instilled in me to be a giver,
not a taker.*

Acknowledgments

To write this book, I drew on the help and support of the many positive, health-conscious people who are part of my life. They believe in me and in the message I bring about what is true health care and how you can achieve it. I especially want to thank the following people:

My wife, Sallie, for being there by my side every step of the way, for giving me her love and patience, and for supporting me in all of my endeavors.

My daughter, Christina, and my son, Nino: may the sun always shine on you both.

My wonderful family and my great extended family. Thank you for your support and encouragement throughout the years.

Joanne Kabak, for being a true professional, for using her great skill and magic with words to help put my thoughts into print. Without Joanne, this project could not have gone so smoothly.

Nicole Traini, for her fantastic drawings, her imagination, and her ability to turn my thoughts and words into art.

Norman Goldfind of Basic Health Publications, Inc., for believing in this project and having the confidence in me to carry it out.

My staff at Delta Chiropractic and the group at the Optimum Health Institute, for being superb colleagues in the work of bringing good health to people.

And a special word to all my patients and the thousands of people I've met on the journey to good health: So many of you have said, "You ought to write a book." Thanks to you, here it is.

Preface

The other day, I was at my daughter's volleyball tournament and I was shouting and cheering like a madman—for everybody. The guy next to me turned and said, "I never saw a parent cheering so hard for both sides!" You know what I said to him? "I encourage everyone. That's the kind of guy I am. I'm the biggest cheerleader in the place." And that's what I want to say to you at the outset of this book. I'm your biggest cheerleader. I may not know you personally, but it doesn't matter. Just like at my daughter's volleyball game, there's no "good" side and no "bad" side. They're all great kids playing their hearts out. When it comes to health, there's no "you're my friend and I care about you" or "you're not my friend, so I don't care if you get sick."

We're all here together on planet Earth and what we do affects others. If you're the pilot on my airplane, if you're a teacher in my son's classroom, If you're a patient in my office, your health affects me personally. And you can be sure I want you to be as healthy as possible. But if our paths never cross and the only way we connect is through this book, I still want you to be as healthy as possible. In fact, I want everyone you know to be healthy, even if they don't pick up my book. How's that going to happen? Because you'll be so inspired, so knowledgeable about health, that you will pass on the information. That's how it works.

That's how we will all end up in a world of health care, not disease care. The world of disease care is expensive and painful, full of anxiety and lost opportunities, and it's full of death before your time. The world of health care is positive, active, doesn't cost extra money, and leads to a long and fulfilling life. That's what I want for you.

I'm a man with a mission—to help as many people as possible lead healthy lives. I love people, I talk straight, and I genuinely care. I'm honest, positive, and optimistic. And I'm a skilled medical professional who understands the human body and the distinction between the good choices and the bad ones.

To the thousands of people who've been my patients or who've come to my lectures, I'm "Dr. Andy"—the guy who listens to them, understands their problems, and gently but firmly guides them on the path to health. Through this book, I'm "Dr. Andy" to you too. I know that sometimes I sound tough. I don't talk to you the way a lot of medical people do. But I don't have unlimited pages in this book, and you don't have a lot of time to read.

So, I want to tell you straight out what you need to know. You need to Stop and Think. You need to adopt the Seven Habits of Healthy Living. You need to get real each and every day about what is going to help your body and what is going to hurt it.

I've been a practicing chiropractor for fifteen years. I've taught everyone about health, from the richest celebrities who could afford anything they wanted to buy, to homeless kids who are too poor to have anything but the basics. Each person has an equal right to know how to live healthily and has the ability to carry it through. Hey, does an apple cost any more than a doughnut? It's all about knowing the differences and the effects on your body—and sticking to making good choices.

Patients come to see me for a lot of reasons, including natural detoxification, weight loss, and stress reduction. I've treated and lectured to people from all over the world. People leave my health lectures with information, direction, and a sense of personal commitment, thanks to the way I present my message. Health is not boring! It's one of the best, most interesting, and, yes, most fun topics in the world.

Above all, I'm an old-fashioned chiropractor. I align the body, encourage harmony, and help people to function at 100 percent of their potential. Chiropractic medicine, the second-largest healing profession in the world, has been saying for decades, "Be careful about drugs, be careful about surgery, focus on wellness." And I'm very knowledgeable about nutrition. Did you know that in chiropractic training, there is ten times more actual class time spent on nutrition than in a typical medical-school education? Every day, I continue to educate myself about the latest studies and research into all aspects of health and wellness, including nutrition. I didn't make this stuff up! I'm just putting it together and telling you in a way that will make you think and take action.

You know, I wasn't born a chiropractor. In fact, I was just like you perhaps—looking for a magic pill, thinking that drugs were really going to make me better and that I didn't have to do anything myself. When I was a young man, I was working two jobs, day and night. One day at work, I got injured. I took the usual route and went to the doctor and got pills for my painful shoulder. When I stopped taking the pills, the pain came back. Then I needed more pills. And so on.

It just didn't make sense to me that popping pills was the way to restore health. My wife, who worked for a chiropractor, told me to go see a chiropractor. So I did. That began a whole new way of life for me. I got better without being in a vicious cycle of pain and pills, then more pain and more pills. I became so motivated by experiencing these better, more lasting ways of healing that I decided to become a chiropractor myself. So, I'm not telling you to do anything I wouldn't do myself. I'm just asking you to join me on the road to health.

CHAPTER 1

Stop and Think

N. Trani

THIS BOOK IS ABOUT PUTTING YOUR BODY IN A POSITION TO WIN. How? Stop and Think. First, I want you to take time every day to stop what you're doing, stop rushing around, stop making the same old choices you always do like you're some kind of robot. Then, think about your lifestyle and your health—ask yourself, "How's my life going? How do I feel today? What am I doing right now to prevent myself from getting sick? How am I making sure I give myself the best chance for a long, healthy life?"

You need to start living your life in health care, start thinking about what you're putting into your body on a daily basis. I know you want to have a life that's long and healthy. Are you even asking yourself what it's going to take? If you're looking for the magic pill, well, there is no magic pill.

There are studies coming out every day telling you what's going to help you be healthy and what can make you sick. But you may not be getting the message. That's what drove me to write this book—I can tell you what you need to know, what you're doing wrong and what you're doing right, encourage you, and cheer you on.

Ask yourself the Stop and Think questions right in the moment: "Why am I still sitting down on the couch? Why haven't I exercised yet today? Why haven't I gone out for a walk, run on the treadmill, ridden the stationary bike?" The new federal guidelines for healthy living say that you should exercise an hour or more every day most days of the week. It's not a secret—it's all over the news. I want you to take responsibility to exercise every day.

Here's another series of Stop and Think questions: "Why am I opening up the refrigerator? Am I hungry? What am I going to do when I open up that refrigerator? Am I opening it just to open it or am I going to stuff the first thing I can find into my mouth?" What you put into your mouth is a big part of the Stop and Think program. Why? Because obesity has become a major epidemic in this country. I want you to take responsibility for what you're putting in your mouth.

My vision of living a healthy lifestyle is to make it simple:

- Stop and Think.

- Understand how your body works.

- Use the Seven Habits of Healthy Living.

- Pay attention to the latest news about health.

- Do everything you can to live a life that's as long and healthy as possible.

- Make it fun!

It's time to wake up. Stop and Think is a program to help you increase your consciousness and guide you to solid knowledge about health. Life is about making choices, good choices. But many people are making poor choices or don't even think about the choices they make. They're just operating on automatic pilot. There is a lot of information out there supporting good habits and healthy living, and it's about time you use that information for your own sake.

It's time to wake up. Stop and Think is a program to help you increase your consciousness and guide you to solid knowledge about health.

Healthy longevity, along with a healthy lifestyle, is the key goal here. Why would you want to work your tail off all your life and all of a sudden, when you get to be sixty-five years old, you find that you can't enjoy your life? What you need to do is Stop and Think about what you're doing right now, how you live your life, and the choices you're making. And I'm going to help you do that.

YOUR BODY: SUPREME BEING ON PLANET EARTH

The human body is the most sophisticated thing known to man. We are the "supreme being" on planet Earth. There is nothing that even comes close. No scientist would dare compare even the most complex technology, such as the space shuttle, with the human body—it's an insignificant toy compared to the body.

If you respect the body as a supreme being, your life and your health will be better. If you disrespect the body—by smoking, drinking alcohol, eating junk food, not exercising—then your "being" is self-destructing. You get sick. So, you grab a pill that maybe makes you feel a little better, but ends up making some other part of you sick because of unwanted side effects. And soon enough, your original problem comes back because you never changed your lifestyle; you just covered up the problem with a pill.

Here's the most important message I'm going to tell you: the human body is a self-healing organism, given the right circumstances. If you don't believe that, you can stop turning the pages. But if you believe the body heals itself, given the right circumstances, then keep reading.

The body heals itself from the inside, not from the outside. For example, if you cut your finger and it begins to bleed, does it heal? Of course it does. To get the cut to heal, did you have to read a book, watch a video, or take a class? No, because the body knows how to heal. It does it every day, twenty-four hours a day, seven days a week. Think about this: every twenty-four hours, the body makes 300 billion new cells. That is absolutely amazing.

Okay, let's continue with the example. Let's say you cut your finger again, but this time, you pick at it . . . pick, pick, pick. What happens now? It gets infected and begins to form scar tissue. Then you cover it with plastic—a Band-Aid. Plastic does not have special healing powers. If plastic could heal, my credit cards would do wonders by now. But if we take care of the body, and give it the right nourishment, it can miraculously heal itself.

We are the supreme beings, hands down. A few years ago, IBM made a computer called the Deep Blue Supercomputer. It was designed to challenge Garry Kasparov, the chess champion who was the best player in the world for sixteen years. Up until then, no human had been beaten by a computer in the game of chess. So, IBM bet Kasparov $400,000 that its new computer could beat him. Why? Because if IBM beats the world chess champion, it can claim to have the most powerful computer in the world.

What happened? IBM lost. The computer they designed calculated over 100 million chess moves per second. Still, the human brain beat the computer. The brain runs the body with 75 trillion cells operating life every single day. This is phenomenal power. This is awesome power.

So, IBM made modifications and then bet Kasparov $700,000 that it could beat the chess champion. This time, IBM finally did it—Kasparov lost to Deep Blue. The machine calculated over 200 million moves per second. That's what it took to beat the human brain in a game of chess, a board game. Just so we're clear on this, that computer couldn't even tie its shoe if it had one!

Because the human body is a supreme being, you want to treat it the best way possible in order to live in wellness. Wellness is a lifestyle. It's also a thought process, something that one makes a choice to do. It's an awareness to live your life in health care versus disease care. To live in health care means to live with vitality, being as strong as you can be all throughout your life. It means maximizing the days that you're on the planet, and the most critical way you can do that is through the choices you make.

Does health care have to be all the time? No. Does it have to be most of the time? Yes. People often say, "Well, the holidays are here. What do I do?" This is what I tell them: "Listen, the holidays are an exception to the rule. Have fun but use moderation. Eat, enjoy yourself, be with your friends and family." That's an important part of our social structure. But the rest of the time, you should follow the rules. The rules are to watch what you do, watch what you put into your mouth, watch how you live your life, and watch how you maintain your environment, making sure that it is a safe, healthy place. Look at the entire environment in which you live and evaluate it as you read this book.

Recognize, too, that sometimes it's not what you're doing but what you're *not* doing that's the problem. In other words:

- You're not exercising enough.

- You're not drinking enough water.

- You're not eating five servings of fruits and vegetables a day.

- You're not quitting smoking.

- You're not controlling alcohol consumption.

The exciting part is that when you realize what you're not doing and change it, you are turning your life around and empowering yourself again. You feel like, "Wow, I can really help myself get better. I don't need medication. I don't need to go to a doctor. I feel vital, and I am motivated and inspired to get healthy."

Do the right things throughout your life and when you reach age fifty, you can feel like life is just beginning. It's even the time when you're reaching your prime! But what happens if you keep doing the wrong things and don't change? All of a sudden your knees are buckling out from under you, you're 40 pounds overweight, and you can't do the things you want to do. You become depressed.

But you can change that outcome. This is the right time to make it happen for you. I tell my patients, no matter what age they are, "This is the perfect time in your life to get healthy." They look at me kind of strangely. I say, "Yes, this is the time to take care of your body, right now. When you're seventy-five years old, you'll be so happy you did!" Remember, when your body is the supreme being on Earth, it is supreme every day it is here, right until the end. It's up to you to keep it in supreme shape. This book will show you just how to do that.

IT'S NOT JUST MY OPINION

Every month, I read numerous wellness and nutrition newsletters and medical journals. Every day, I read the newspaper for the latest health

news. "Okay," you say, "you're a doctor, you've got to do that for your practice." And you know what I say to you? You've got to be reading and listening too—you're a human being and you've got to do it for your own health.

Listen, all the facts I tell you about lifestyle, diet, and disease and how to stay healthy are not just my opinions. They come from clinical research studies—from the United States government and from universities around the world. It's all available to you, but are you seeing and hearing it? And are you acting on it?

As I'm writing this book, the news headlines are about the prescription drug Vioxx being taken off the market because it can cause heart problems. New concerns are appearing almost every day about other painkillers as well. As you're reading this book, there are probably a bunch of new stories and new studies and new dangers in the headlines. This information is vitally important to your health. Pick a newspaper, magazine, wellness letter, or website, and read it regularly to see what's going on. Start doing it today.

Throughout this book, I mention research that's important to the health topic being discussed. There are thousands of additional examples out there. I can only tell you a few. This information may come directly from a research study, or sometimes it appears in the local paper. This health information isn't hidden. What you need to get and stay healthy is right in front of you, if you learn to pay attention. After all, it's not my opinion—it's scientific fact.

For example, you've probably heard that five servings of fruits and vegetables per day can help prevent colon cancer, rectal cancer, stomach cancer, and lung cancer. Where did that information come from? The American Cancer Society stated it in 1996. They said eat five or more servings of a variety of vegetables and fruits each day. They didn't say *one* piece of fruit or *one* side of vegetables at dinner; they said *five* servings. What does that look like on your table? A half cup of broccoli is a serving; a single orange or an apple is a serving. Do you get the picture of how much of these foods you should be eating every day? Are you doing it?

If you want to know why it's so important, just look at a report that came out in 1997: *diet is responsible for 40 percent of all cancers.* The American Institute for Cancer Research and the World Cancer Research Fund analyzed more than 4,500 clinical studies and found that diet has a profound effect on cancer risk.[1] Researchers found that 20 percent of our current cancer incidents could be eliminated if everyone consumed five servings of fruits and vegetables per day.

Now Stop and Think about it. Would you rather eat two oranges, an apple, a handful of grapes, and a mango shake each day with a half cup each of broccoli, zucchini, peas, cabbage, and carrots, or would you rather get a diagnosis of cancer? The studies are pretty clear that you really do reduce your risk if you follow the guidelines. What more do you need to know?

But it doesn't look like people are paying attention. In 1998, another study reported that "Americans eat more fruits and vegetables and grains than twenty-five years ago." However, "cancer researchers say one-quarter of those vegetables are french fries."[2] What's the matter with french fries? They have a lot of fat and not many nutrients. Where's the broccoli, the carrots, the kiwi?

In that same year, results were published from an eight-year study of nearly 44,000 men by the American Heart Association, which found that foods rich in potassium and related nutrients may help reduce the risk of stroke. What are good sources of potassium? Bananas, tomatoes, spinach, and oranges.

Do you see a pattern here? If you're eating five servings of fruits and vegetables per day, you can help protect yourself against several forms of cancer as well as strokes.

In the 1990s, studies found the first direct evidence that the same nutrient that makes tomatoes red (lycopene) may protect men against prostate cancer by shrinking the tumors and slowing their spread. That news confirmed a study from the mid-1990s released by Harvard University that looked at the eating habits of 47,000 men over six years. Those who had at least ten servings weekly of tomato-based foods were up to 45 percent less likely to develop prostate cancer.[3]

If you didn't know this before, you're getting the picture now. When you get one piece of evidence after another, you know the truth's in there.

And there's more evidence: "Fruits and vegetables may cut the risk of breast cancer in premenopausal women who have a family history of the disease," according to researchers at the Harvard School of Public Health, who have studied the diets of more than 83,000 women in the Nurses' Health Study since 1980. By 1994, 2,697 of the women had been diagnosed with invasive breast cancer. The key finding: among premenopausal woman who had a mother and/or sister with breast cancer, those who reported eating at least five servings of fruits and vegetables a day had a 70 percent lower risk of breast cancer compared to those who ate less than two servings per day.

Why do you think that is? Because nature makes the apple perfect; nature makes broccoli perfect. Stop messing with it! Don't try to substitute when you can have the real thing. Just eat it!

These few studies have shown us a lot so far. If you're eating five servings of fruits and vegetables per day, you can help protect yourself against colon cancer, rectal cancer, stomach cancer, lung cancer, strokes, prostate cancer, and breast cancer. I know I'm repeating myself—this time I really want you to hear it, remember it, and act on it.

But what's happening despite the fact that all this scientific evidence is coming out? Obesity is on the rise. People aren't paying attention. You know, broccoli and apples don't make you obese, but french fries do. According to a 2000 study, "52 percent of Californians are overweight. Despite the healthy tofu-and-avocado image that Californians enjoy across the country, more than half the state's adults are overweight."[4] What's worse is that the percentage is up from

44 percent in just ten years. We're going in the wrong direction!

Here's one of the biggest reasons to pay attention to your diet. A recent study says that if you gain weight, the risk of cancer increases too. The World Health Organization's Cancer Agency said that up to one-third of cancers of the colon, breast, kidney, and digestive tract are related to weight gain and not getting enough exercise. If you put on weight, even if you're in the normal range, your risk increases.

Staying healthy is about how you live your life day in and day out. It's about the choices you make right now.

When you get to the Seven Habits of Healthy Living later in the book, remember these studies and reports. It's not just my opinion; it's the opinion of the major researchers around the world. And they're telling you the same kind of basic information in study after study.

Staying healthy is about how you live your life day in and day out. It's about the choices you make right now.

CHAPTER 2

The Ferrari:
A Wake-Up Call

LET'S TAKE A FERRARI AND A VOLKSWAGEN—WE'RE GOING TO HAVE A RACE, five miles straight. You're going to bet everything you own—your dog, your fish, your house, your money—on which car you think would win. Would it be the 2005 cherry-red Ferrari Testarossa or the 1967 lemon-yellow VW Bug? You'd put it all on the Ferrari, right? However, what if we put soda pop in the Ferrari's gasoline tank and we give the VW Bug a super-grade gasoline? Which would you put your money on now? The Volkswagen, of course!

Well, we're all living in the Ferrari right now. You have the most awesome machine known on Earth—the human body. If you learn one thing from this book, let it be this: if you feed your body better, it runs better; if you feed it crap, it runs worse. That's as complicated as it gets. What illusion are you living under? If you give a Ferrari poor fuel, you expect it to run poorly. However, if you feed your body poorly, you somehow expect it to run well. Why do you think that? Don't!

Of course, when it's time to go get some gasoline, do you rush to ABC gas? No, you pass by all the cheaper gas stations and get only the best gas for that car. Only the best! But when you're hungry, what do you do? "Oh, look, a 99-cent hamburger!" You drive right into the fast-food joint and pick up a cheap hamburger, right? I've seen people do it. Do you know that we pay more for gasoline than we do for lunch? We're out of our minds!

Have you thought about those 99-cent hamburgers? For the fast-food joint to make any money at all, that hamburger cannot cost them more than 50 cents to produce. And with that 50 cents, they have to pay for counter workers, product liability, rent, cleaning, gas and electric, and so on. So, what do you think you're getting? There's a name for it—it's called junk food!

> You have the most awesome machine on Earth—the human body. If you learn one thing from this book, let it be this: if you feed your body better, it runs better; if you feed it crap, it runs worse.

If I took two dimes and threw them on the ground, you probably wouldn't go pick them up. So, why do you run after a few cents when a fast-food place throws them at you? The food chains have price wars to suck you in. It reminds me of a cartoon I saw. A skinny guy behind the counter at a fast-food place says, "Our fries now have 50 percent less fat." The customer, who weighs about 300 pounds, replies, "Great! I'll take two!" That's the problem! The hamburger is now 99 cents, so you order two or more of them! Or you "supersize" your french fries for 39 cents. Do you want to make your belly bigger for 39 cents, because they're going to give you more fat, more salt, more artificial colors? You're not going to get more tomato, more onions, or more lettuce.

Look, I sound very tough when I talk about junk food and about people ignoring the basic facts of how to be healthy. But I'm not saying this to put anyone down. That's not what this book is about. This book is about how you should live your life.

If you're going to go pick up something to eat, don't run to a fast-food place. Go to the grocery store and get an apple, an orange, a banana, or some squash or broccoli. Get some real food. Don't eat junk, because that's when you poison your Ferrari.

Are you making the connection between what fuel you put in your body and the state of your health? Or are you more like Mr. Smith here?

Doc Andy: Hi, Mr. Smith, how are you?

Mr. Smith: Oh, I'm a mess.

Doc Andy: What's wrong with you?

Mr. Smith: Doc, I catch the flu every season. I get every cold. My blood pressure is through the roof. My cholesterol is out of control. My back is killing me and I can't even golf anymore. I'm a disaster.

Sound familiar?

Doc Andy: Wow, that's pretty bad.

Mr. Smith: It is pretty bad.

Doc Andy: Well, you know, Mr. Smith, why don't you tell me about your day, how do you live your life? The little routine when you get up in the morning, what is it that you do?

As a health professional, I have only so much time to spend with you, so I'm going to get all the information I can out of you. I might role play with you, agree with what you have to say, to get you to tell me the truth. You know what you do when you go to the doctor. It's a classic game: you don't tell the doctor anything and wait to see if the doctor can find "it." If he does, then he's a good doctor, right? Pay attention to how I role play with Mr. Smith, how he prevents his body from healing.

Doc Andy: Mr. Smith, talk to me, what do you normally do when you get up in the morning?

Mr. Smith: I make a pot of coffee.

Doc Andy: Oh, you drink the whole thing?

Mr. Smith: Yup.

Doc Andy: So do I!

Mr. Smith: Then I go to McDonald's.

Doc Andy: Which one?

Mr. Smith: The one across the street from here.

Doc Andy: The same one! How come I've never seen you there?

Doc Andy: How about lunch?

Mr. Smith: Oh, I love pizza.

Doc Andy: With extra cheese?

Mr. Smith: You know it's the only kind to have!

I can see we're bonding already. I can feel it.

Doc Andy: What about dinner? What do you eat for dinner?

Mr. Smith: Oh, I have frozen dinners. With the vegetables.

Doc Andy: You ever sweat?

Mr. Smith: Nah. Only when the Chargers keep losing.

So, how is he damaging his health? From what he's putting down his throat, and by not doing the things that would give his body the energy it needs to heal. The problem is not coming from your body; it's coming from your head. The body wants to heal, but what's it getting? A pot of coffee, pizza, frozen dinners. Or maybe it's smoke, alcohol, and glow-in-the-dark food. See how the day goes? So, we put junk food into our Ferrari and then wonder why we're losing in the race for living a long and healthy life.

Do you think because you're not bleeding on the outside that you're not bleeding on the inside? We do bleed on the inside. When my boy was little and scraped his knee, he'd cry, "Dad, I'm bleeding." He can see he's hurt. But when you bleed on the inside, no one sees it. Everything's okay, right? Well, everything is not okay.

Do you know when you find out? After you get sick: a heart attack, a diagnosis of diabetes, a bad cold. Instead of worrying about if there's enough flu vaccine, worry about whether or not you're doing everything you can to build up your immune system. Why not feed your body healthy food and be strong all year long so you can resist any cold or flu? A weak body is going to be susceptible to all these bugs.

N.Trani

Think about the Ferrari with the soda pop and the VW with the good gas. Who's going to win the race? When it comes to getting the flu, who's going to have a better chance to fend it off, the person with the strong immune system or the one with the weak one? It's time to wake up to reality.

THE ONE SCENARIO

As a practicing doctor for the last fifteen years, I've had the opportunity to meet people from all walks of life—different cultures, different economic statuses, different ages—and from all over the world. I work with the elderly, children, athletes, office workers, you name it. One absolute constant that I find is that each person ends up telling me why it's okay to do something that isn't good for his or her health. It's what I call the "one scenario."

A patient comes in for an examination, and I begin by asking some basic questions to find out what's going on.

Doc Andy: Do you drink coffee?

Patient: Yes, I have one cup a day.

Doc Andy: Oh, okay, what else do you have?

Patient: Well, I like to drink a soda a day too.

Doc Andy: Just one?

Patient: Yup, just one.

Doc Andy: Okay, what else do you like to have?

Patient: I like to have a hamburger a day too.

Doc Andy: Just one hamburger?

Patient: Just one.

Doc Andy: Any french fries with that burger?

Patient: How'd you guess? I also have an order of french fries. Just one order.

Doc Andy: And what else do you have throughout the day?

Patient: Well, I like to have a candy bar.

Doc Andy: Just one candy bar?

Patient: Yeah, just one candy bar.

And then I ask about what happens when the patient gets home.

Doc Andy: Well, what do you do when you get home? What else do you like to have?

Patient: Well, I like to have a martini.

You know my next question.

Doc Andy: Just one martini?

Patient: Yeah, just one martini.

Doc Andy: What else? Do you like to have dessert? A piece of pie?

Patient: Yeah, I have a piece of pie also.

Do you see the situation here? Do you recognize the "one scenario"? It's all an attempt to justify why it's okay to have whatever you want—a justification clause. You justify it because you're only having one of something. But by the end of the day, you have twenty of these "ones." All twenty have entered your body. The "one scenario" is probably one of the most health-destroying concepts that people have come up with.

I'm asking you to look at your whole lifestyle, to pay attention throughout the day to what you're actually eating. Stop and Think about the "one scenario." Are you truly having just one food that you know is harmful to you or are your "ones" actually adding up to a lot of food that could cause big problems?

How many "ones" would you add up in a month? How many would you add up in a year? What about in the past five years? And you want to know why it is that you develop a health problem!

I'm reminded of the "one scenario" whenever I watch a football game. I've got my favorite teams, and I love to watch them. But what else do I see? Beer commercials, one right after the other. Many of them claim that their beer is low in calories. Why does that matter? Are they trying to tell me it's a healthy beer? No! What they're really saying is, "Go ahead and drink more than one. You can even drink five or six. You don't have to worry about getting a beer belly from our beer!" These commercials are sneaking through the back door to get you to make a mental note that if you drink more than one beer, the calories won't add up. It's like giving you permission to drink as many as you want! The message is subliminal. You need to be able to pick up on that, and you've got to be careful. It may be disguised but it's still the "one scenario"—the justification clause—at work.

> Stop and Think about the "one scenario." Are you truly having just one food that you know is harmful to you or are your "ones" actually adding up to a lot of food that could cause big problems?

If you keep justifying your behavior this way, eventually, something shows up—your blood pressure begins to change or your cholesterol levels creep up. I ask you the question, "What's changed in your life?" And you say, "Nothing's changed. It's always been the same. That's the way I always do things." Right? You have one of everything and by the end of five years, you add that up and you've got thousands upon thousands of things that have entered your body. If you take into consideration one candy bar a day for a year, that's 365 candy bars. Add a soda, that's 365 cans of soda. Keep adding—365 hamburgers, 365 pieces of pie . . . and on and on. This happens all day long. I want you to know that it is not an aberration or a weird case. This happens to be the lifestyle of most people today. It may be you, reading this book right now.

The "one scenario" is absolutely one of the most dangerous things we practice, because it adds up with time and it wears our bodies down. It's a kind of trick we play on ourselves so we can justify unhealthy behaviors. Stop and Think about what you're doing. There are no good excuses for unhealthy behavior, and it's time to wake up and take responsibility for your own well-being.

CHAPTER 3

Digestion
Made Simple

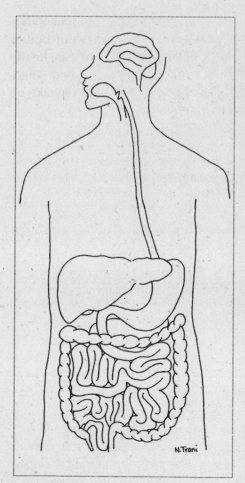

N.Trani

BEFORE GETTING INTO THE SEVEN Habits of Healthy Living, it's important to look at digestion and how it affects the major systems of the body and your overall health. Adopting a healthier lifestyle can have a major impact on how well the body functions, thus preventing many of the most common illnesses.

THE DIGESTIVE SYSTEM

When was the last time you studied the digestive system? High-school biology class? Unfortunately, too many people just don't know how foods, liquids, and drugs get processed and flow through the system. It's not a matter of something going in one hole, through some dark hidden passageways, and then out another hole. There's a whole lot more going on in there!

I'm going to tell you about digestion and the gastrointestinal (GI) tract in just a few pages. I'll go fast, but I'll go over it so you really understand what you need to know. I'm going to share with you what I tell my patients. I'm going to ask you to Stop and Think about the key steps of digesting and eliminating whatever you put into your body. It is part of understanding why you need to follow the Seven Habits of Healthy Living.

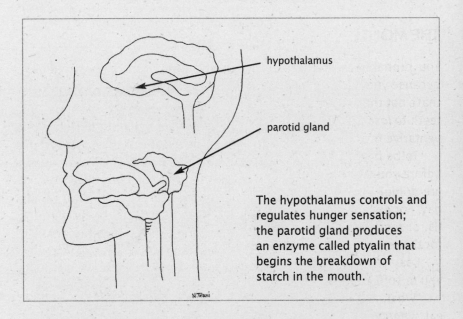

hypothalamus

parotid gland

The hypothalamus controls and regulates hunger sensation; the parotid gland produces an enzyme called ptyalin that begins the breakdown of starch in the mouth.

N.Trani

If I asked you where digestion starts, some of you might say the stomach, others would say the mouth. You would be wrong on both counts. As the above illustration shows, digestion actually begins in the brain. The nervous system controls and coordinates all the functions in the body. In other words, when your mouth starts to water and you're all excited about food, that's coming from your brain. We experience the hunger sensation in the brain in a place called the hypothalamus. In fact, the hypothalamus is probably speaking to you right now: "I'm hungry, I'm hungry, I'm hungry. . . ."

Why is this important? It's all connected. This is a key point to remember about digestion. (In fact, it's a key point to remember about everything that goes on in your body.) What happens in your brain and your nervous system directly affects what goes on in the rest of your body, and that includes the stomach. For example, your body normally produces about 10 milliliters (ml), or 0.34 ounces, of hydrochloric acid in your stomach. Individuals with chronic levels of stress can produce up to 50 ml (1.69 ounces) of hydrochloric acid, due to the overstimulation of the brain, which affects digestion. That's five times the normal amount, meaning that high levels of stress for long periods of time can produce gastric ulcers.

THE MOUTH

You probably think that you brush and floss your teeth every day because you want a beautiful smile. Sure, that's part of the reason, but that's not the main reason. You brush and floss because you want your teeth *to last*. That's good dental hygiene but, most importantly, it's preventative medicine.

To be healthy, you need to chew your food twenty to thirty times before you swallow to mechanically break it down. Is this what people are doing? I don't think so, not from what I hear from patients every day. For example, Mr. Jones has lost a lot of his teeth. He's got gingivitis, or tooth decay. I give him an exam, and he comes back in a week for the results.

I say to him, "I know what's wrong with you. It seems to me that you're suffering from malnutrition."

"What, are you nuts?" Mr. Jones exclaims. "I own a grocery store. I eat *whatever* I want, *whenever* I want. How could you say I'm malnourished?"

I have to tell him how it is. "Mr. Jones, when you smile it's Halloween every day for you. You have lost the ability to mechanically break down your food properly. You therefore have lost the ability to absorb it correctly. Over a period of years, you have entered a state of malnourishment." That's exactly what happens.

The next patient is Mrs. Jones, and the visit goes something like this:

"What do you eat, Mrs. Jones?" I ask.

"Well, I *don't* eat apples," she replies.

"Oh, you don't *like* apples?" I ask. But I already know what's going on in her mouth.

"No, I *do* like apples," she replies. "It just hurts to eat them, so I don't."

This is just another way that people become malnourished. They begin to avoid certain wholesome foods, like apples, because it hurts too much to eat them.

Here's another good reason to take care of your teeth: more than 600 species of bacteria live in the mouth and around the teeth. That's bad enough, but research shows that the bacteria don't just stay in the mouth—they migrate to the rest of the body and invade the bloodstream and various organs. Perhaps the health of the mouth is a big clue to the health of the rest of the body. Taking care of your teeth and mouth gives you an inexpensive, effective way to prevent serious illnesses like heart disease.

If you keep your teeth healthy, you have a better shot at keeping the rest of your body healthy. It's just common sense. Please take care of your teeth now: brush and floss them every day. This is the very first step for good digestion and good health. You'll be getting a beautiful smile along the way too!

Now, pick up a mirror and look inside your mouth, under the tongue, and over by the jaw. What do you see there? Glands. The sublingual glands are underneath the tongue and the submandibular

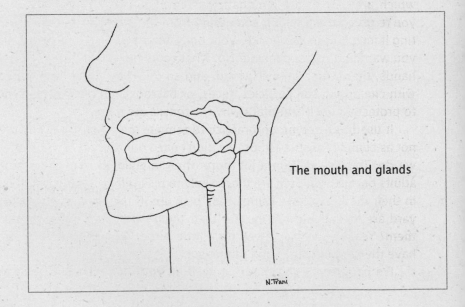

The mouth and glands

N. Trani

glands are by the jaw. What's so important about them? These two sets of glands are primarily responsible for providing salivary juices to help process the foods you eat. It's hard to eat with a dry mouth, correct?

The other gland you need to know about is the parotid gland. It squirts out an enzyme called ptyalin that begins to break down the starch in your mouth. Up to 5 percent of the starch you eat is broken down in your mouth by ptyalin.

So, in the mouth you have a mechanical breakdown of your food via your teeth and an enzymatic breakdown of food by the enzyme ptyalin. But how much ptyalin are you going to mix in the food when you eat too quickly and don't break down foods enough—clump-and-swallow, clump-and-swallow, clump-and-swallow? Not much, I'm afraid. You end up sabotaging yourself because even though you may eat plenty of food, you're not getting the nutrients out of it.

When you say, "Oh, no, I can't eat any more. I can't even breathe," it means you're in too much of a hurry. What state of mind should you be in when you eat your meal? You should be relaxed and calm. Slow down, be calm, and chew thoroughly.

THE TONSILS AND APPENDIX

If you look all the way in the back of your throat, you'll see the tonsils, which are part of the lymphatic system. Look, all through the day, you're going to be taking something from the *outside* world and putting it into your *inside* world—your body, your own supreme being. Do you want to dirty it up inside? No. What could be dirty? Start with your hands, then water, utensils, food, and so on. They could be polluted with chemicals, soil particles, feces, or bacteria. You need something to protect yourself and that's why the tonsils are there.

It used to be common practice to remove the tonsils, but now it's not as common. In the 1960s, we didn't need our tonsils. In the 2000s, we do. Tonsils swell up a lot more often in children than they do in adults because children are more likely to pick things up and put them in their mouths. Those things they pick up off the floor or out of the yard are loaded with germs. Do their tonsils go to work and protect them? Yes. Maybe they swell up a little bit? Sure. Maybe you should have them pulled out? I don't think so.

I'm here to tell you that you need all your body parts as long as you can keep them, whether or not you know what they're for. If you didn't need them, you wouldn't have them. There's no extra carry-on baggage in the body. All the bags are packed and loaded on because you really need them for the trip of life.

And that applies to the appendix too. You often hear people say, "Oh, the appendix is useless." Not so. The appendix plays a role in fighting off bacteria, pathogens, and foreign bodies as they enter the large intestine. So, actually, the appendix and the tonsils play a big role in the lymphatic system to filter out harmful substances as they pass through the digestive system.

THE ESOPHAGUS

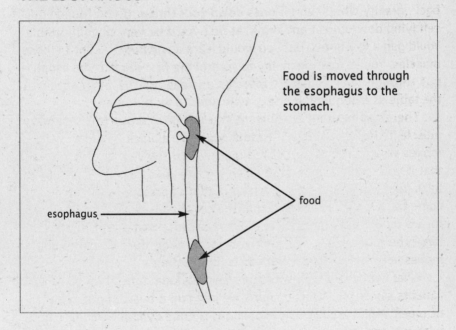

Food is moved through the esophagus to the stomach.

food

esophagus

The esophagus extends from the bottom of your jaw to the middle of your chest, the mid-sternum. It's the food tube—liquids and solids all go down it on the way to the stomach.

The first third of the esophagus is made up of striated or voluntary-type muscle. It is controlled through the conscious mind. If I tell you, "Lift your hand," you can pick your hand right up. That's your voluntary muscle at work. However, the body has another type of muscle called smooth or involuntary-type muscle. The last two-thirds of the esophagus is made up of this type of muscle, the same kind that surrounds most of the organs in your body. The subconscious mind controls this system.

Why has nature made the esophagus so that we can control the first third, but not the next two-thirds? It's a survival mechanism. Have you noticed that when a baby's born, he or she is upside down? When the baby starts nursing, he's lying sideways but he doesn't choke. Ever watch a baby in her crib, lying down, face up, sucking on a bottle of milk? The baby doesn't choke.

As you grow up, you're not eating like a baby anymore. You sit up, swing your food and drink into your mouth, the tongue slips the food back, gravity works, and it goes down your throat. If you found yourself lying down to eat and drink, at first you'd be very uncomfortable. You'd gag a few times, but you would learn again how to control those muscles. You've lost the ability to control the first third of the esophagus through your voluntary muscles. Instead, you've been sitting at the table as a good adult and gravity goes to work for you.

There's something else I want you to know about this voluntary muscle in the first third of the esophagus—it's a quick-acting muscle. It moves very fast, but it gets tired quickly too. You've probably noticed that if you cough after you've eaten a meal, your food does not come back up. Even if you sneeze, which is a lot of pressure, food does not come back up. The reason is that the esophagus can stay contracted for up to six hours after a meal. Why? Because that smooth, involuntary-type muscle that we can't control through our conscious mind moves very slowly. Its contraction is long lasting.

What happens if the esophagus isn't working right, if it's diseased? Patients say to me, "Doc, couldn't we just pull it out and put in a plastic pipe?" Well, we can't. The esophagus is quite dynamic—contracting, relaxing, and contracting again. We don't have the technology to do that with synthetics. That's why we need to protect our esophagus.

Let's take a closer look at the area. You have two tubes in your throat—the esophagus and the trachea, the air tube. You breathe and speak through the trachea. What separates the two of them is a flap in the rear of the throat called the epiglottis. If you say a few words right now, your epiglottis is going to flip over, cover up the food tube, and let the air tube stay open to put air into the lungs. When you swallow, the epiglottis covers the air tube and lets liquids and solid food go down the food tube into the stomach. So, what happens when you're talking and eating at the same time—talking-chewing, talking-chewing, talking-chewing? The epiglottis is confused! The flap flips out! And you can choke.

So, what state of mind should you be in when you're eating your meals? You know the answer by now: relaxed, calm, and quiet. Chew your food thoroughly, swallow it, and then talk. Stop talking, then put food in your mouth, and chew some more.

The Antacid Machine

One of the biggest injustices to your digestion in America today is what I call the advent of the antacid machine. I'm talking about drugs like Pepto-Bismol, Pepcid AC, Rolaids, Tagemet, Nexium, and all the rest of those little pills and liquids. I'll tell you why I'm so angry about them.

Perhaps you've seen this commercial: a guy says, "I can't eat my mother's chicken cacciatore because when I eat it, it gives me heartburn." Now I'm an Italian kid at heart and my ears perked up. *The guy can't eat his mother's chicken cacciatore? What's going on? What's the guy going to do?* Here's the answer in the commercial: take a little pink pill. His mom is happy now because her son is eating her chicken, and the guy is happy because he's eating without heartburn. No one has to change anything, right? Problem solved! I don't think so.

Another commercial shows two women in the drive-through at a fast-food restaurant, with the kids screaming in the back of the van.

Mom #1 says to the other, "Have some onion rings."

Mom #2 replies, "Oh no, I can't have those because when I eat them, it gives me heartburn."

Mom #1 says, "Just take this little pink pill."

And what am I thinking while this little story is going on? Sure, take the little pink pill, so you can eat all the crap you want. Isn't that what the commercial is saying?

Are these people getting healthier or sicker? The answer is obvious: they're getting sicker. Why? Because no one's asking the real question: "Hey, why can't you eat your mother's chicken cacciatore in the first place?" His body is telling him that it hurts him to eat it, but he's not listening. What about the woman at the fast-

Next, let's take a look at peristalsis, the waves of involuntary con-tractions that move food and waste products along inside the gastroin-testinal tract. Once food gets into your system, you don't have to say, "Move!" It just happens without your thinking about it. We have three major peristaltic movements a day to process the three major meals a day. How the food moves through the esophagus is very different from how it moves in the small and large intestines. In the esophagus, the stuff you swallow goes straight through to the stomach.

Sometimes you may suffer from heartburn. Of course, you know

---

food joint? Her body is actually screaming that the onion rings hurt her, but she's not paying attention either.

What about you? Are you paying attention to your body or to the commercial? Who's teaching you about drugs? The television! Commercials paid for by the com-panies that made the drugs. Do you think that's a way to get all sides of the story? Listen, I'm not anti-medication or anti-surgery, when you really need them. I have tremendous respect for the medical community. What I am against is abuse of med-ications and medicating yourself instead of understanding your body and making healthy choices.

Let's look at the problems of chronic heartburn in a different way. After you eat certain things, you feel like you're burning up inside. So, what do you do? Your first instinct may be to fill up on medication. The problem is that pink pill is a drug. It's going to disrupt your digestive system and force your liver to detoxify your body. It's not going to fix the underlying problem of why you get heartburn from chicken cacciatore or onion rings in the first place.

Any time you take drugs or medications, do it because it is the lesser of two evils. There is nothing inherently good about drugs going into the human body. However, sometimes drugs are *necessary*. What I'm trying to tell you is that drugs and medications can help something, but they also hurt something else. I really want you to understand this. They upset the natural balance in your body in some way. You should take a drug only when you really need to and there's no other natural option.

You need to realize that if you're experiencing heartburn regularly, you've got a problem going on in there that you need to take care of before it gets worse. Reaching for the pills is what I call living your life in disease care. I'm telling you how to live in health care by truly caring for your own body.

your heart is not burning, right? So, what is burning? The inside of the esophageal wall is burning from too much acid. A damaged esophagus can lead to esophageal ulcers or gastroesophageal reflux disease (GERD). Ulcers can put a hole in your esophagus. In your stomach, there's a mucous lining (about a sixteenth of an inch thick) that protects it from the high levels of acid. If that lining wears away, the stomach is exposed to acid and you get ulcers.

The esophagus doesn't have that thick mucous lining, so it's exposed. If acid comes back up from the stomach, which is what happens in GERD, it goes directly into the esophagus and there's no protection. The acid disrupts the wall of the esophagus, and the more it happens, the more it continues to burn holes. You end up with mutations to the wall. In the worst-case scenario, you could burn a hole right through the esophagus, and undigested food could start leaking through.

If you have chronic heartburn, several times a week, don't just let it continue to happen. Find out why and fix the cause. Otherwise, you may develop a health opportunity you just don't need—the opportunity to have an ulcer.

THE STOMACH

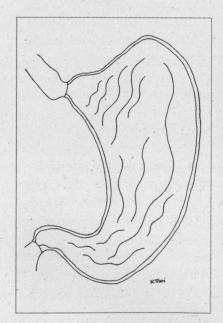

Think of the stomach as a blender. Its job is to break everything down—fats, proteins, complex carbohydrates, sugars, and starches. You do not feed the body through the stomach. What does cross through the stomach membrane quite easily are water, aspirin, and alcohol. Each of them quickly gets absorbed right into the body.

Let's look at water first. The human body is approximately 75 percent water. Would nature want water to go anywhere it can go in the body? Yes! So it makes sense for water to be absorbed through the stomach.

Aspirin is one of the most effective drugs of all time, because it crosses the stomach membrane and goes straight into the blood-stream. It's very effective. The problem is that it's got side effects, particularly gastrointestinal bleeding. That's why you have coated aspirin, time-release aspirin, and alternatives to aspirin. It's very hard on the gut lining. Did Mother Nature plan on aspirin going through the stomach membrane? I don't think so.

How do we know that alcohol crosses the stomach membrane quite easily? Think about what happens when you take a shot of tequila: it goes right to your head. Pharmaceutical companies know this—what do some medications for cold symptoms have in them? Alcohol, of course. Those medications do not take care of your stuffy nose. When you take a shot of a cold medicine, you don't feel your nose anymore—you're intoxicated. Now, someone's going to argue that's not the way it works. Believe me, this is one of the ways that these medicines work. In commercials, they're called "nighttime medicines." That's because if you take them, you're going to go to bed—they knock you out.

From the esophagus, food comes down to a one-way valve called the cardiac sphincter, which allows the food to go into the stomach. Now, why is it called the cardiac sphincter when we're speaking about your stomach? The stomach and the valve are located near the heart. This has clinical significance because indigestion can mimic a heart attack, and a heart attack can mimic indigestion.

Pressure on this valve can actually feel like the pressure you have with a heart attack. Now, when you feel the discomfort, nine times out of ten it's indigestion. However, when you have discomfort in this area, don't roll the dice and think it's not a danger sign. It can be, so be sure to have it checked.

I want to tell you two stories with very different endings. Both of them are about elderly patients. One didn't make it back on Monday, and the other did.

With the first patient, who had frequent indigestion, I kept insisting that he go back to the hospital and be checked, and checked, and checked. When he didn't make his Monday morning appointment, I was worried about him. Unfortunately, he had a heart attack and died.

The other patient came in one day, and I asked how her weekend was.

"I had that feeling again," she said.

"What happened?" I asked.

She replied, "I went to the hospital, they checked it out, and I'm all normal."

"Then what's the deal?" I wanted to know.

She thinks she's figured it out. She's an eighty-year-old woman and she tells me, "I eat fast food at a taco shop on Fridays and it gives me heartburn."

I couldn't believe what I was hearing. "Wait a minute—what are you doing eating spicy fast food? You're eighty years old! What are you doing there?"

She's got to make some changes in what she eats. But because she had symptoms, she at least went to the hospital and checked it out. In her case, they figured out it was heartburn and sent her home. The first patient had symptoms too, but he did not return to the hospital to be checked out again as I instructed him to do. If you have burning pressure on your chest and you're not feeling good, realize that it's not necessarily heartburn all the time. This is when you should Stop and Think. Your body's talking to you and you need to listen to it.

At the end of the fundus, which is the body of the stomach, there is the pyloric valve. This valve allows the food to enter the small intestine. In the stomach are squiggly things called gyri or rugae. I like to call them gyri. Think of your stomach in a resting state like a water balloon with everything squeezed out of it. As you fill it with water, it needs to expand. The gyri allow it to do that.

In the gyri, there are cells called oxyntic cells, which make hydrochloric acid, the juice that actually breaks down your food. There's another substance the gyri make called mucus. The stomach has a one-millimeter lining of mucus to protect it from the high levels of acid you're producing. That's a very dense lining. The oxyntic cells also make a protein called intrinsic factor, which I will talk more about later.

Other cells in the stomach are called chief cells, which make pepsinogen. When pepsinogen interacts with hydrochloric acid, it then becomes pepsin. It's the pepsin that breaks down the protein in your stomach.

The pH scale, which measures acidity and alkalinity, goes from 0 to 14, with higher numbers being more alkaline. When you have food in your stomach, it becomes an acidic environment. Everything starts to get broken down. But as the broken-down food goes into the blood-stream, it's going to change quite dramatically from acid to alkaline. Items like baking soda or sodium bicarbonate are very basic, or alka-line, and they're at one end of the spectrum. Water is neutral; it's in the middle. The acidic environment of the stomach is at the opposite end of the spectrum, with a pH of 0.8 to 1.38. The acid level in the stomach is so strong that it could burn a hole in a carpet. It could even make a hole in a penny.

So, the oxyntic cells make hydrochloric acid, mucus, and intrinsic factor. Intrinsic factor's job is to go out and find vitamin B_{12}, which is important for the maturation of red blood cells. Without intrinsic fac-tor, we would not be able to absorb vitamin B_{12}. The only other way to get this vital nutrient into the bloodstream is to inject it or to take a liq-uid supplement placed under the tongue where the sublingual gland will absorb it. The way it works in the normal digestive process is that intrinsic factor finds vitamin B_{12} in the small and large intestines, grab-bing the vitamin in what's called a lock-and-key bond in biochemistry. Anytime you hear that, understand that once the bond is locked in, you can throw away the key. It's a really strong bond. Next, vitamin B_{12} goes to the liver and gets stored. How much vitamin B_{12} do you need a day? About 5 micrograms (mcg) is the recommended daily allowance (RDA). The liver stores about 4,000–5,000 mcg. A lot more than you need each day!

So how does this play out in real life? Mrs. Smith comes into my office. "Ugh! I'm a mess, Doc Andy," she tells me.

"What's wrong with you, Mrs. Smith?" I ask.

"For a month now, my legs feel like they weigh two hundred pounds. I wake up tired, and everything's double the effort. By the end of the day, I'm totally fried and can't get up from the couch. *Some-thing's wrong with me!*" she wails.

What do you think she hears from me? "Mmmm, I see. Have you been sick? Have you changed your diet? Have you moved? Did you have the flu? Get a new job? Change your exercise routine?"

"No, no, nothing's changed," she replies. "*Something's just wrong with me.* "

"Okay, Mrs. Smith. Here's what we're going to do. We'll do some lab work. You come back in a week. Maybe we can find out what's going on."

A week passes and she comes back. I have an answer for her. "Mrs. Smith, I know what's wrong with you. You have what they call *pernicious anemia.*"

"What's that?" she wants to know, of course.

So I explain to her that her red blood cells are not maturing properly and are dying prematurely. "It's usually caused by a deficiency in vitamin B_{12}."

Right away she asks, "Should I take B_{12} injections? Or B-complex vitamins?"

"Well, for the short term that might help," I tell her. But then I go on. "What I want to know is what changed in your life about five years ago? You see, Mrs. Smith, it would've taken you four to five years to deplete all of the B_{12} in your liver."

I know that Mrs. Smith hasn't had this problem for six months, one year, two years, three years. She's had this problem for *four to five years.* And now that she has the symptoms, here she is in my office.

Health care is for every single day of your life. This is health care, not to be confused with disease care or crisis care. You end up in the hospital, you have a crisis situation. Believe me, they're patching you up any which way they know how. That's 100 percent disease care. I'm going to give you an example. It's sort of a negative story, but it's real-life stuff, so I'll share it with you. Don't worry. You'll see how this story is related to our discussion of the stomach.

I have a patient. He's forty-two years old. A virus attacked his heart muscles. It's called a cardiomyopathy. In other words, his heart muscle was dying on him. Call it bad luck, bad timing, being at the wrong place at the wrong time. I have no idea what to call it. All I know is it happened to him. (By the way, if you met him today you wouldn't even know he was ever sick. He's doing great. He no longer carries a transplant pager, and he's no longer waiting for a heart transplant. The medication worked. We know sometimes medication is necessary. The heart attack or the pills? Obviously, we'll take the pills. It's the lesser of two evils.)

So anyway, the day after I found out about his heart condition, I went to the hospital to see him. Remember, he was a man in heart failure. What were they feeding him? A roast beef sandwich, a cup of Jell-O, and soda pop! "Man, what are you doing?!" I asked. "Why are they bothering to give you a new heart? They're killing you with this!"

Now, if real health care were going on, would they have been feeding him that, do you think?

We mustn't forget that it's all connected! Your heart isn't in some box ten miles away from your stomach and intestines. Don't make this mistake. Instead, I want you to make good choices, starting with your brain. The choice you make with your brain affects what you put into your mouth. What you put in your mouth affects your throat, your esophagus, and so on. What travels through your digestive system spreads throughout your entire body. Like I said, it's all connected. So let's keep on going down the digestive path.

THE PANCREAS

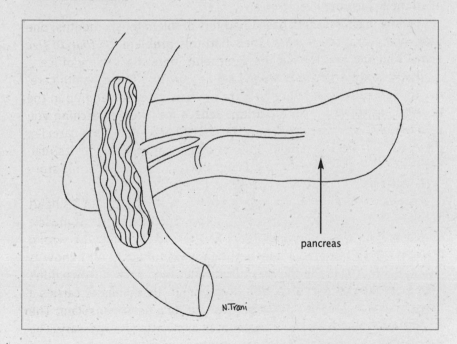

pancreas

N. Trani

When you think of the pancreas, what do you think of first? Insulin production and diabetes, right? However, when it comes to digestion, the pancreas is a major player. Why? Because it produces digestive enzymes. The pancreas is an organ that looks like a piece of corn and is located near the duodenum, the first part of the small intestine. The pancreas produces digestive enzymes that break down food in the small intestine: trypsin and chymotrypsin break down protein, amylase breaks down starch, and lipase breaks down fat. For this reason, the pancreas is an important part of the whole digestive process.

THE LIVER AND GALLBLADDER

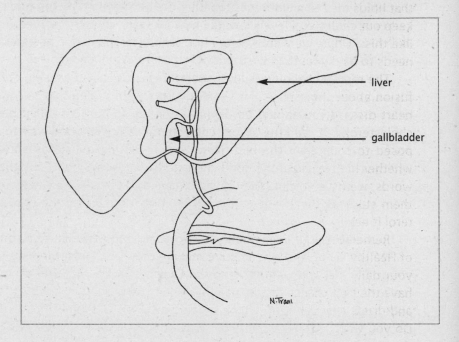

If I were to list systems and organs of importance in the body, it would go like this: the nervous system, your brain—number one; the cardiovascular system, your heart—number two; the detoxification system, your liver—number three. The liver is high on the list of organs and for a very good reason: the liver is the major detoxifying organ of the body, the one that cleanses your blood. The liver has two lobes, the right lobe and the left lobe, and it is a regenerating organ, given the right circumstances. In fact, you can destroy up to 75 percent of the liver and not skip a beat. In a way, that's to our detriment in making choices for a healthy lifestyle. You can end up living a lifestyle that eventually wears you down, as way too many people do, and not realize that you're damaging the liver. You don't see it or feel it until you are already well along the road to disease.

The liver performs more than 700 functions every day. One of those functions is to produce bile, which breaks down the fat in your food. Another function is to produce cholesterol. Without cholesterol, you could not survive. Commercials for cholesterol-lowering medications don't tell you that. Cholesterol is a gooey, membranous material that holds the cell membranes together. So, after years of being told to keep our cholesterol levels low, the new message might go something like this: "Oops, we were wrong about cholesterol levels. Cholesterol needs to be *higher* than we thought."

The rapidly changing field of clinical research is also causing confusion about cholesterol. For years, doctors were saying that to treat heart disease you should be paying attention to both so-called bad cholesterol, LDL, and the "good" cholesterol, HDL. The good was supposed to counteract the bad. Now, they're raising questions about whether high levels of the good cholesterol are always good. In other words, we have no clue. Here's what I have to tell you: Who cares? Let them study all they want—the body is going to make all the cholesterol it needs.

Remember your liver when you're reading about the Seven Habits of Healthy Living and when you're making choices in each moment of your daily life. You want to keep the liver healthy so all parts of you have the best chance to stay healthy. When you put toxins like alcohol and drugs into the body, which organ is working overtime? The liver. Do you want a drink? Drink, have a good time, but know that you're destroying one of the most important organs in your body. It is not a game, and you get away with nothing. You take a toxic material, you put it into your body, and it doesn't just come out the other side. Your body now has to deal with it.

If you live a certain lifestyle, your liver is going to be affected. I want you to understand from the beginning that the habits I recommend don't come out of thin air. They are rooted in what you need for your liver and for every other part of your body so you will be healthy all over. But the liver plays an especially important role in keeping you healthy.

Now, the liver produces bile, but bile is stored in the gallbladder. It's the gallbladder's job to concentrate the bile ten times. During the digestive process, the gallbladder sack squeezes, bile enters the intestines through the bile duct, and fat gets broken down. That process is called the emulsification of fat.

Gallstones are generally seen in individuals with a chronic high-fat diet. If that sounds like you, what do you have to produce in sufficient quantities to break down the fat? Bile. What organ makes the bile to begin with? The liver. What else does the liver make? Cholesterol. So, cholesterol comes along for the ride—it serves no purpose in the actual breakdown of your food, but it can sit in the gallbladder. If it sits there long enough, it will precipitate and become a gallstone. If a gallstone comes out and lodges in the bile duct, you then have a medical emergency. You do not need chiropractic time, acupuncture time, massage time, green tea time, or yoga time. No! You need surgery time. Because now you can die. If you have a crisis situation, you have to go to a specialist or to the emergency room and get it taken care of.

Now, this situation will not happen from eating one french fry, but it will happen with a lifestyle of constantly eating french fries. Every year, 800,000 gallbladders are removed because of a crisis situation.

It goes like this all too often: After the crisis and the ensuing surgery, the patient arrives in my office and says, "Gallbladder's gone. No more problem! Now I can go back to eating what I want!"

I hand him a business card for the cardiologist.

"I don't have a heart problem," he says.

"Not yet," I reply. "But if you keep eating the same way you did before, you will. Without your gallbladder, your body can't break down the fat. The fat is going to go right to your arteries and veins. In about two to three years, you'll have heart disease. You might as well take the card now."

Don't wait until you have the symptoms, the pain, and the big medical bills. Why bring that on if you don't have to? Think about your liver and gallbladder when you make your choices. When you look at that bottle of wine, that bag of fatty french fries, Stop and Think.

THE SMALL INTESTINE

The small intestine is actually where the body feeds itself. In fact, 90 percent of absorption of food takes place in the small intestine. And it has a lot of space to do it in: the small intestine is 22 feet long.

If nature chose the small intestine to send food through to the rest of the body, you better believe the small intestine is important and is well equipped to do the job. What does it need? It needs as many points

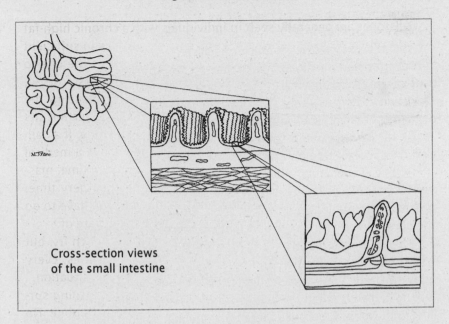

Cross-section views
of the small intestine

of contact as possible to get food through to the body. It has millions of microvilli to do this job. If you could take one square inch of small intestine and spread it out, the surface area would be a couple of square feet. If you spread out the whole small intestine, the surface area would cover an entire tennis court!

When the food is going through the small intestine (and the large intestine as well), it's moving in a corkscrew action, creating agitation—it's like a washing machine. No kidding. The body is made in the best way possible to do the job of getting nutrients through.

Along with all the work that the small intestine is doing for digestion, it's also playing other important roles in the body. It's helping keep the body free of toxins and infections. It's one of the major places where the digestive system comes together with the lymphatic system, the cleansing system of the body.

Now, here's another important aspect of the small intestine I want you to know about. In the first part of the small intestine, the duodenum, there are glands called Brunner's glands that produce more mucus. When the mucus kicks in, it elevates the pH in the area to 5.38. When that happens, the cells that were making acid in the stomach, the oxyntic cells, shut off. They're not happy in that pH environment.

The pancreas also helps break down the acid with its digestive enzymes and some help from sodium bicarbonate ions.

As I told you before, the nervous system controls and coordinates all the functions in the body. It has two responses: a sympathetic response and a parasympathetic response. The sympathetic response is known as fight or flight. That's when you're scared, you're either on the move or facing your "attacker," you're sweating, maybe you're running—the body is being stimulated with adrenaline. The parasympathetic response is the opposite; it's the calming side.

You can't run a marathon and eat a meal. When you try to do that, your blood is focused on only the parts involved in running: legs, arms, and back. It's not focused on digestion. When we're calm and relaxed, the parasympathetic side is dominant. That's the digestion side.

The Brunner's glands work on the calm, parasympathetic side. When you run a marathon and eat a meal, what is going on in your body to protect you during digestion? Who is going to turn on the Brunner's glands when the acid from the stomach goes into the small intestine? Nobody, because there isn't any mechanism there to protect you from that acid. That's why 50 percent of all ulcers are duodenal, occurring in the first part of the small intestine. Eat a meal and run a marathon and you'll get one.

That's why you need to be in a calm, relaxed state of mind and body when you eat your meals. You have to understand that this is a survival mechanism. Back in the days when we were cavemen and cavewomen, if we were picking some berries and a bear showed up, we didn't say, "Excuse me, I'm eating now." No, we ran for our lives. You know that you've got to run and you just go. But the jungle has changed: it's out there on the freeway. I see people talking with one hand and eating with the other. I have no idea who's driving! So, the message is, you need to be calm and relaxed when eating. That's how the digestive system is set up to work.

THE LARGE INTESTINE AND COLON

Does a high-fiber diet reduce your chances of getting colon cancer? Yes! A high-fiber diet provides bulk and roughage to keep wastes moving through the large intestine. Look at the average American diet: cheese, pizza, hot dogs, hamburgers, french fries, ice cream, candy,

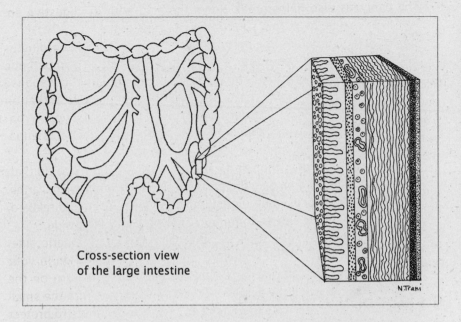

Cross-section view
of the large intestine

cookies—the "glow-in-the-dark" food! Basically, that's one big crappy situation.

Remember how the peristaltic action moves food through the small intestine and large intestine? It agitates and pushes the food through in a corkscrew action. What do you need to do to get things started? Put food in your mouth, chew twenty or thirty times, and swallow. That's the hardest part! There are cells on the surface of the large intestine and small intestine called the crypts of Lieberkuhn. They produce a mucosal lining that protects the intestinal walls from the remaining acid in our stools. So, when the waste product goes twisting around, it doesn't rub up against the intestinal wall and cause ulcerative colitis. A high-fiber diet (several servings of fruits, vegetables, and grains per day) cleans everything out.

When you have a low-fiber diet, fecal matter remains in the intestine and can become impacted. Your body wants to get rid of it so it begins to absorb it. That causes diverticulitis. A high-fiber diet will throw it out. There's another kind of food—one that's healthy for you—that could pose a problem here: seeds and nuts. They can also get impacted in the large intestine, so eating a lot of seeds and nuts without a lot of fiber and water could become an irritation. Even with seeds and nuts, we still need vegetables, roughage, and water to help clean us out.

One final point: the health of the digestive system has an effect on the health of the immune system. In the digestive system, the very acidic environment of the stomach can kill bacteria. In the small intestine, the lacteal ducts protect you by keeping pathogens and toxins from going into the bloodstream. So, how you treat your digestive system can have a profound effect on your overall immunity. And isn't that one of the things that will be most helpful in getting you through life as best as you can, a strong immune system? If your digestive system is weak, everything eventually starts to break down. On the other hand, if you eat well, your body builds up a healthy atmosphere in every part. Later in the book, I'll provide detailed information on how to improve your diet to keep your digestive system running smoothly and efficiently.

IT'S ALL CONNECTED

The digestive system, cardiovascular system, nervous system, musculoskeletal system, and immune system are all related to one another. I've gone into the digestive system in detail so you can see how it works. I hope this chapter has helped wake you up about what is going on inside your body. This also lays the groundwork for understanding why the Seven Habits of Healthy Living are so important to your health. I didn't make them up because they sound good—I put them together because they are important for your gut, your heart, your liver, and the other body systems. They are the habits that help make all parts of the body hum along like a well-oiled machine.

> Health care is not for just this week because you're reading this book. It's not for the week after, when you finish the book, or even the week after that. Health care is for every single day of your life.

I wish that just by telling you how the body works, you would be so excited and so convinced of how to live well that you would change all your bad habits to good ones. Health care is not for just this week because you're reading this book. It's not for the week after, when you finish the book, or even the week after that. Health care is for every single day of your life.

Health care is not to be confused with disease care or crisis care. If you end up in the hospital, you have a crisis situation and they're going to patch you up any way they know how. That's 100 percent disease care, which has nothing to do with health care. Reading a book like this and following through on its recommendations has everything to do with health care.

I want you to make good choices, starting with your brain. A calm state of mind can have a profound effect on your health. The choices you make affect what you put into your mouth. Then that affects your throat, your esophagus, and on down. And what goes through the digestive system gets spread throughout your entire body. The nervous system, digestion, the musculoskeletal system, the lungs, and the heart—like I said, it's all connected.

CHAPTER 4

Habit Number One:
Don't Smoke

I HAD AN INTERESTING CONVERSATION WITH A PATIENT THE OTHER DAY. She told me that she loves to smoke and that she's been smoking for thirty-nine years. How does she justify that? She said she smokes "good quality" cigarettes and that somehow they're clean, they don't have the carcinogenic chemicals associated with smoking. That's how she came to the conclusion that she was smoking "a healthy cigarette." So, I said to her, "You want me to tell you that's okay? I'm not going to do that. In fact, I'm going to tell you definitely, categorically, it's not okay." I gave her a lot of reasons why there's no such thing as a "healthy" cigarette, and I'm going to give you those reasons too.

The number-one cause of preventable death in the United States is tobacco related. According to the U.S. Surgeon General, 440,000 people die each year from conditions that are due to tobacco use. Not only that, smoking-related health problems cost approximately $157 billion per year in economic losses. It is estimated that, since the first Surgeon General's report on smoking was published in 1964, cigarette smoking has caused 12 million deaths.[1] In spite of all the public awareness of the problems associated with smoking and recent declines in smoking rates, more than 46 million Americans still light up. And each day more than 4,000 young people smoke their first cigarette.[2]

Smoking harms just about every organ in the body, causing disease directly and reducing health in general. Smoking contributes to a long list of cancers. Lung cancer, of course, is first: in 2003, it was expected that lung cancer alone would kill 157,000 Americans.[3] Smokers are twenty times more likely to get lung cancer than nonsmokers. But there is a causal relationship between smoking and other types of cancer as well: breast, esophageal, pancreatic, bladder, cervical, leukemia, and stomach cancer.[4]

One study found that by smoking just a pack of cigarettes, you can absorb 2–4 micrograms of cadmium. There seems to be a direct link between low-dose cadmium exposure and an increased risk of breast cancer, according to researchers at Georgetown University. This is due to cadmium's ability to mimic the hormone estrogen in the body and affect cell growth.[5]

But the disease list doesn't stop there! Smoking also contributes to heart disease, chronic lung disease, low bone density, peptic-ulcer complications, erectile dysfunction, and cataracts. You increase your risk of dying of heart disease fourfold by smoking. Even hip fractures are more common in smokers than nonsmokers! Smoking may also lead to reduced fertility in women; pregnant women who smoke have an increased risk of low-birth-weight babies and children with damaged lungs or congenital malformations.[6] And low-tar or low-nicotine cigarettes are no safer for you.

Smoking is not only harmful to you directly—secondhand smoke can cause health problems in those around you. "The hazards of secondhand smoke, a known carcinogen, are no longer disputed even by the tobacco industry. Scientists say secondhand smoke can cause cancer, heart disease, and intensify other respiratory conditions such as asthma."[7] California state lawmakers have proposed legislation that would fine motorists if they smoke with children riding in the car. "KIDS IN CAR? THEN NO SMOKING, BILL SAYS" was the headline in the *San Diego Union-Tribune.* "Kids are particularly susceptible to secondhand smoke, particularly younger kids," said Assemblyman Marco Firebaugh. "They are still growing and secondhand smoke is very harmful to them."[8] You love your kids, your family, and your friends. Why would you ever do something that you know could cause them to get cancer?

QUIT SMOKING NOW

If there's any good news in this, it's that scientists say for each year that passes since kicking the smoking habit, your risk of dying from lung cancer drops. So, the sooner you quit, clearly the better it is. One study found that how long and how many cigarettes you smoked, as well as how long it's been since you quit, make a difference in your chances of getting lung cancer. There's actually a formula for smokers and ex-smokers over age fifty to use to calculate their own risk. For example, a sixty-eight-year-old man who has smoked two packs a day since he was eighteen and is still smoking has a one-in-seven chance of getting lung cancer by his seventy-eighth birthday if he keeps smoking. If he quits, the risk drops to one in nine.[9]

Quitting smoking reduces your risk of other smoking-related diseases as well:

- The risk of getting cancers of the mouth and throat are halved in five years.

- Heart disease risk is reduced by 50 percent in one year.

- The risk of ulcers, chronic lung disease, and bladder cancer all drop after quitting.[10]

So, quitting smoking has both immediate and long-term health benefits. Your general health will greatly improve if you quit. Smoking harms your immune system and increases your chances of getting infections—quitting can help in both of these areas.

If you haven't gotten the point by now, listen to this: On July 1, 2005, the Centers for Disease Control and Prevention reported that smoking reduces life expectancy an average of fourteen years. Why? Because you get lung cancer, heart disease, and other illnesses. A lot of people say, "I'm going to party, I'm going to smoke. So what? I'll live to be ninety. It's only going to cost me six months of my life." Not true! The scientists are telling you that when you smoke, you lose *years* off your life. Not three months, not six months, not one year. *Fourteen years!*

> This is a choice
> that you, the smoker,
> are making. No one is
> forcing you to smoke! You
> are putting yourself in this
> predicament. Stop and Think
> about what you're doing. Quit
> smoking now. And if you're
> not a smoker already,
> *don't ever start.*

This is a choice that you, the smoker, are making. No one is forcing you to smoke! You are putting yourself in this predicament. Stop and Think about what you are doing. Quit smoking now. And if you're not a smoker already, *don't ever start.*

Now, I realize it's not easy to quit. But your health, maybe even your life, depends on it. Find a program that works for you and stick with it. You know, most smokers try to quit several times before finally succeeding, so don't get discouraged. However, the longer you stay away from cigarettes, the less likely you are to reach for the pack again.

Different methods work for different people. You may have to experiment to see what works best for you. For example, some of my patients have tried hypnotherapy with success. Here are a few suggestions for helping you to quit smoking:

- See your doctor or healthcare professional regularly while you are trying to kick the smoking habit.

- Join a support group and get friends and family on board your program to quit smoking.

- If you feel the desire for a cigarette, find some healthy snacks to nibble on instead. A lot of people are orally fixated and they grab a cigarette to satisfy that need. See "Bowls and More Bowls" in Chapter 8 about placing snacks that are good for you around your house.

- There may be some weight gain after you quit smoking, but this is usually only about 5 pounds or so. Eat a well-balanced diet during this time to keep gains to a minimum. Starting to exercise will help as well.

- Don't give up!

CHAPTER 5

Habit Number Two:
Don't Drink Alcohol

N. Tran

DON'T DRINK! WHY SHOULDN'T YOU DRINK ALCOHOL? Like smoking, alcohol affects just about every organ and system in the body. It affects the liver, pancreas, brain and nervous system, stomach (it erodes the inner wall of the stomach), and the cardiovascular system, where it causes vascular fragility. That is, the capillary beds in the body begin to break down. In fact, chronic alcoholics often have a reddish nose. What's happening is that the capillary beds in the nose are weakening, allowing blood to leak out of the capillaries. Take that image and think about what else is going on inside your body with chronic alcohol use.

The risk of getting cancer increases with higher levels of alcohol use, particularly cancers of the esophagus, liver, breast, and prostate. Hepatitis C and other chronic liver diseases are made worse by drinking alcohol.[1]

Because it is so prevalent and considered socially acceptable, drinking alcohol is thought by many to be a harmless vice. Unfortunately, this is simply not true by any stretch of the imagination. Alcohol consumption has both an enormous health cost and a significant social cost.

It is estimated that almost 55 percent of American adults drink alcoholic beverages at least once a month. About 33 percent of adults in the United States report binge drinking (five or more drinks on one occasion), and almost 6 percent of adults are heavy drinkers (more than two drinks per day for men, one drink per day for women).[2]

There are also the social problems that alcohol use brings with it, such as problems in the home and danger when people drink and drive. Alcohol use is related to increased levels of crime, domestic violence, and risk of sexually transmitted diseases.[3] In 2001 alone, there were 1.4 million arrests in the United States for driving under the influence (DUI).[4] How many accidents happen when people drive under the influence of alcohol and they actually end up killing people? In 2002, more than 17,000 people in the United States were killed in alcohol-related car accidents.[5] If you choose to drink, do not drink and drive, ever.

That's why it's best not to drink. Alcohol is hard on the body and it can harm the lives of others.

I get this question quite often: What about a glass of red wine with meals? Studies have shown that a glass of red wine with meals is good for the heart and for digestion. Red grape seed extract is the greatest antioxidant known. It helps against free-radical damage, which among other things benefits the heart. Therefore, the connection has been made that red wine is good for the heart. The problem is that we may think, "Hey, if one glass of red wine is good, then two is better." Right?

Be careful with that scenario. Some studies say half a glass of red wine would be just as effective and other studies suggest that grape juice would give you the same benefit as red wine. That being said, an argument can be made that, yes, a glass of red wine with meals is beneficial. However, don't use that as an excuse to consume the whole bottle. Stop and Think about what you're doing and be responsible.

Here's a true story. A patient came into the office for an exam. He filled out a health questionnaire, which I looked through before his exam.

Doc Andy: You indicated here that you drink. So, what do you drink?

Patient: I drink wine.

Doc Andy: Okay. How much do you drink?

Patient: Oh, ten bottles.

Doc Andy: Ten bottles? Is that a year?

Patient: No, that's a week.

Doc Andy: You drink ten bottles of wine a week?

Patient: Yeah. Why? Is something wrong?

Doc Andy: Well, isn't that a lot?

Patient: You're kidding, Doc. Everyone I know drinks wine. You don't?

Doc Andy: No, not really.

See, I'm the weirdo now. Listen to what he's saying: "Everybody I know drinks wine." Here comes the justification, when someone tells you it's okay to do something unhealthy.

Patient: By the way, I don't drink the hard stuff anymore.

Doc Andy: Oh, I see, it's okay to drink ten bottles of wine a week because you don't drink the hard stuff anymore, right?

Be careful about the justifications. That's how unhealthy habits sneak up on you. A glass or two of wine a day, a few bottles of wine per week—it starts to add up.

By the way, this patient is a CEO of a multi-billion-dollar company. He wines and dines all over the world on business trips. So, he's very successful in his professional life, but when it comes to his health, he is going down the tubes. When that guy retires, he *really* retires. He's done.

Be careful about the justifications. That's how unhealthy habits sneak up on you. So, be aware of how you're affecting your lifestyle when you say, "Oh, no big deal." A glass or two of wine a day, a few bottles of wine per week—it starts to add up. Don't drink even one bottle in a year, and the glasses will add up to zero. Your liver, your brain, your nervous system, and your heart will thank you for it.

For help, Alcoholics Anonymous has a long track record, true and proven—start there. For more information on other types of support or treatment, ask you doctor, healthcare provider, or do research on the Internet.

CHAPTER 6

Habit Number Three:
Don't Take Drugs

BY DEFINITION, ALL DRUGS ARE CONSIDERED A POISON. Why? Because they alter normal human physiology.

Conventional medicine, including the use of pharmaceuticals, often does more harm than good. A recent report from the Nutrition Institute of America, called "Death by Medicine," provided some startling statistics:

- Over 2 million people per year have adverse reactions to properly prescribed drugs while in the hospital.

- Over 7 million medical and surgical procedures are performed annually.

- Almost 9 million people are unnecessarily hospitalized every year.

- Conventional medical treatment causes over 750,000 deaths per year.[1]

In spite of this, more people are taking drugs today than ever before. This is why it is so important to Stop and Think, to do everything you can to stay healthy and avoid the conventional medical system as much as possible.

DRUG SAFETY AND EFFECTIVENESS

The truth is we don't know if the drugs we take are safe, even if they're out in the marketplace. Here's what the *New York Times* said on its front page on December 6, 2004: "Drug companies test their products in people before they are approved, but sometimes potentially serious problems arise only when they are being used by millions of people. . . . [A]lmost everyone, including critics, outside drug safety experts, medical journal editors, some industry executives and even top agency officials, now agrees that [the FDA's] mechanisms for uncovering the dangers of drugs after they have been approved is woefully inadequate. . . ."[2]

> The truth is we don't know if the drugs we take are safe, even if they are out in the marketplace.

You should write that out and paste it on your medicine cabinet. The experts are telling you that they don't know if a drug will cause a health problem for you even if it's been approved. The message: please be careful. Know what the adverse reactions are and know what you're doing. These things are dangerous, so be careful about taking drugs. Don't take them unless you absolutely have to; that means you take a drug only when it is the lesser of two evils.

There was a recent study on acetaminophen, the scientific name for Tylenol, which is in about 200 products and certainly considered safe by most people. How many hospitalizations are due to acetaminophen toxicity every year? According to scientists at the Food and

Drug Administration (FDA), more than 56,000 emergency-room visits each year are due to acetaminophen overdoses. About one-fourth are unintentional—people may not realize they are getting multiple doses from different products—and there are about 100 deaths each year, although that number is probably underestimated. It turns out that overdoses destroy the liver.[3]

In a recent newspaper interview, Dr. Allen Roses, Senior Vice President of Genetics Research at pharmaceutical giant GlaxoSmithKline, states, "The vast majority of drugs only work on 30 or 50 percent of the people."[4] In fact, in most of the clinical studies showing how well a drug works for a specific condition, 50 percent effectiveness is considered a phenomenal success. Most drugs work for a far lower percentage of people, even in the drug company's own studies, but these drugs are still marketed as cure-alls. So, drugs are not only often harmful, but many of them just don't work for most people.

THE "OOPS SCENARIO"

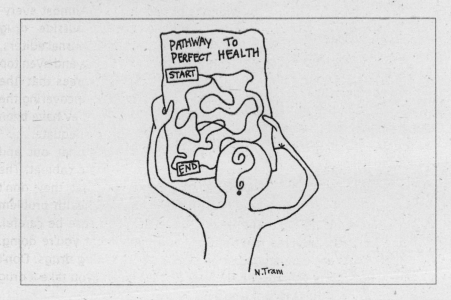

Anytime you hear what I call the "oops scenario" in medicine, there's a problem. A few years ago, there was a big "oops." A lot of people lost weight by taking Fen-Phen, which contained pseudoephedrine. Unfortunately, in some of those people, the drug damaged a heart valve and they died. Listen, if you take a pill and in a short time you lose 30 pounds, you should know something's wrong. I don't care if it's natural, supernatural, unnatural, green, blue, purple, square, or rectangle—it doesn't matter. Something has to give.

Another big "oops" was HRT, hormone replacement therapy. After HRT had been used by thousands of women for decades, the government decided to do a study to see if it worked and if it was safe. But the Women's Health Initiative Study was halted by the government in July 2002 because of serious side effects. It turned out that HRT didn't do everything it was supposed to do. It actually hurt women. The long-term effects of hormone replacement therapy (using Premarin and Provera) showed that the hormones had almost no benefit for menopausal women or on heart disease and stroke. In fact, HRT actually increased the risk of cardiovascular problems as well as breast and ovarian cancers in those using them.[5]

In another disturbing example, the FDA announced that common antidepressants may cause some patients, particularly children and teenagers, to become suicidal. So, our children are at risk as well. Drug companies had conducted studies, which they kept secret, that seemed to indicate a link between antidepressants and suicides. Ironically, the studies also showed that antidepressants were generally not effective in helping depressed teens and children.[6] Unfortunately, children are being given antidepressants in larger numbers than ever before, and at younger ages. Both Prozac and Zoloft are widely prescribed and extremely profitable drugs. Are we developing a society of drug-addicted children?

One more recent "oops" was Vioxx. I'm sure you remember it, especially if you were taking Vioxx when they pulled it off the market. In 2004, the pharmaceutical company Merck announced that it would stop selling its arthritis drug Vioxx. When they made the announcement, about 2 million people worldwide were taking it. They pulled it from the market because a study found that it doubled a patient's risk of heart attack and stroke.[7] Merck did $2.5 billion in Vioxx sales in the previous year. It had been widely marketed as a "safe drug" and hailed as an alternative to aspirin (which can cause ulcers and gastrointestinal bleeding). When they took it off the market, it was the largest drug recall in history. Since it arrived on the market in 1999, 84 million prescriptions of Vioxx had been filled. Again, "oops"—we didn't know that these drugs caused these problems.

What about the people who have been taking this drug for the last five or six years? What do you tell them: "Oops, we didn't know"? Again, don't take drugs if you don't have to. Be absolutely certain that the drug is really necessary and find out as much as you can about whether it can harm you.

In defense of the pharmaceutical companies, they put out a new drug after they test it and get government approval. But the drug has not yet been used in a wide population, so they haven't seen the long-term effects of the medication, when a lot of people take it over a long period of time. The problem is you are taking them—you're the guinea pig, the scientific animal that ends up testing whether or not the drug is really safe.

> If you're looking for the magic pill, well, there is no magic pill. You need to start living your life in health care, start thinking about what you're putting into your body on a daily basis.

BE CAREFUL

Why do we use so many drugs even though we know they have risks? One of the reasons is that drugs are marketed to us like candy. There's a commercial showing a woman exercising. She's vegetarian, fifty-plus years old, and the mother of three, and her cholesterol level is 234. What does she need? Lipitor! Zocor! She's in good shape, but her cholesterol's a little high. Who is the market they're going after? They're after you! Medication is necessary—that's the message they're trying to sell you.

If you're looking for the magic pill, well, there is no magic pill. You need to start living your life in health care, start thinking about what you're putting into your body on a daily basis. Be careful about taking any kind of drug. Let me repeat that, by definition, all drugs are considered poisons and will alter normal human physiology. Stop and Think if that's right for you. Is it absolutely necessary to take a drug? Literally, your life could depend on your answer.

Of course, sometimes you may need drugs to help you heal. But we are living in a time when there's a rush to medicate. Be sure to approach medication that you take as a prescription or over the counter with caution. The first thing to do is talk to your physician. These are typical questions that you should ask him or her:

- How long has this drug been out?

- What are the known side effects?

- How long do you expect me to take this medication?

- Are there any other patients I could speak to that have been on this medication?

- Are there any natural alternatives that would work as well—for example, what if I change my diet, exercise more, or reduce the stress in my environment?

You need to ask these types of questions. Drugs in some cases have serious side effects. In your body, they fix one thing and destroy another. Basically, you may end up at zero.

Besides asking your doctor, look up information that's available to you through websites, articles, and books. And don't just look up the medications. If you're diagnosed with a certain disease process or condition, you can get on the Internet and interact with people all over the world who have the same problem—find out what they've done to heal, what they've tried for natural alternatives, or if they know of any other approaches that might be less invasive than having to take medication.

These are things to think about before you get engaged in long-term use of any medication. Remember Vioxx and many other drugs have been approved by the FDA, put on pharmacy shelves, prescribed by doctors, and taken by millions of people. They hurt a lot of people they were supposed to be helping and had to be withdrawn from the market. Take medicine when you really need it and be sure you find out all you possibly can before making the decision to take it.

I want to help you stay away from drugs, from having the symptoms of poor health that send you looking for a magic pill in the first place. If you live your life in health care versus disease care every day—by following these Seven Habits of Healthy Living—you will be on the path to vibrant health without the use of drugs.

CHAPTER 7

Habit Number Four:
Exercise

I DON'T KNOW HOW ELSE TO EMPHASIZE THIS POINT TO YOU, other than to tell you straight out: you have to get on an exercise regimen. Before you sit down and turn on that TV, I want you to Stop and Think. Ask yourself, "Have I exercised enough today? Have I walked enough? Have I gotten on my stationary bike? Have I taken the dog for a walk?" Bottom line—you have no business sitting down and watching TV until you take care of yourself first. And that means you better get off your rump and go exercise.

Why? Obesity is going through the roof. More than 60 percent of the population in the United States is obese or overweight, according to the National Institutes of Health. It's even affecting our kids: 15 percent of our children from ages six to nineteen are now overweight. Worldwide, one billion people are considered overweight, and 22 million children under the age of five are overweight. It's an epidemic!

> You better get up, Stop and Think about what you're doing, and get a routine going. You need to get out of the habits that are making you become the "blimp."

Every year, new studies show the health benefits of exercise for preventing numerous health problems, including heart disease, diabetes, and osteoporosis. You better get up, Stop and Think about what you're doing, and get a routine going. You need to get out of the habits that are making you become the "blimp."

Life is motion. Let's look at a stagnant pond. What does the water need to do? It needs to be moving. What happens to the water when it's stagnant? All the life in it starts dying. What does the earth do? Spins. If the earth stops spinning, we're toast. So, what do you think the cells in your body need to be doing? What do you think the blood needs to be doing? What do you think you need to be doing? *Moving.*

There are two things that increase longevity—one is exercise and the other is attitude! Your attitude and exercise routine will help you live longer and increase your vitality. If you're not moving, you're degenerating. You've got to exercise. The sad fact is that only about one-quarter of adults get the recommended amount of daily activity, according to the U.S. Centers for Disease Control. What's even worse is that almost one-third of adults are completely sedentary, not moving at all!

Exercise benefits your body physically, but it also benefits your mind. Exercise prompts the release of mood-lifting hormones, which relieve stress and promote a sense of well-being. Repetitive muscle contractions, which take place in yoga, walking, swimming, or other athletic pursuits, increase the level of the brain chemical serotonin, which combats negative feelings. There's also reason to believe that physical exercise might have a positive impact on a number of mental illnesses, including sleep and eating disorders, dementia, substance abuse, personality disorders, depression, and anxiety.

The benefits of exercise may sound too good to be true, but I'm going to tell you this: science confirms that exercise improves your health and can extend your life. Remember, life is motion.

STARTING AN EXERCISE PROGRAM

The first question to ask yourself is, "How much should I exercise per day?" The most recent government guidelines suggest one hour or more of exercise a day most days of the week. That's double the previous recommendation. However, it does not have to be an hour at a time. It can be thirty minutes in the morning and thirty minutes in the evening. Research has shown that people who exercise for short intervals in multiple sessions get the same health benefits as people who like long workouts.[1] You just need to be moving.

Now, for those of you who exercise so you can burn calories, here are some guidelines. If you do four thirty-minute sessions of moderate-intensity exercise each week, you burn about 600 to 840 calories. If you do five to seven thirty-minute sessions of moderate-intensity exercise each week, you burn about 750 to 1,470 calories. However, the best situation, under the latest health guidelines, is to do five sixty-minute sessions of moderate-intensity exercise per week. If you do that, you'll burn about 1,500 to 2,100 calories each week.

Even everyday activities such as walking the dog or taking stairs instead of the elevator can help you get your daily exercise:

- Walking the dog for thirty minutes burns 125 calories.

- Walking through the mall for one hour burns 240 calories.

- Raking leaves for thirty minutes burns 150 calories.

- Washing/waxing the car for sixty minutes burns 300 calories.[2]

Some people think of exercise only as a way to play the "calorie game." That's fine if it motivates you and helps you stay within a healthy weight range. But it's not the only reason for exercising. Here are the real benefits of exercise:

- It keeps your body in shape.
- It exercises your heart and your lungs for increased cardiovascular health.
- It keeps your muscles toned and moving.
- It keeps your joints from getting stiff.
- It makes you sweat, so it helps detoxify your body (sweating is one of the ways the body eliminates toxins).
- It clears your mind and reduces stress.

Look, there's nothing better for the body than exercise. You know this, even if you don't know all the scientific details. But what are you saying to yourself? "I hate to jog. I can't afford a treadmill. I'm horrible at tennis." You pick one or two exercises that you can't do and say, "Well that's it, I can't exercise." That is no excuse! Get rid of that negative thinking immediately! There are so many ways to exercise. Any person, anywhere—and that means you—can find things to do that are true exercise, easily available to you, and that don't cost more money than you can afford.

Here are some of my favorite recommendations. Take a look at this information and then make a list of your own favorite activities. I want to make something very clear to you here. Before you start an exercise program, check with your doctor or healthcare provider and make sure you're able to take on whatever it is you choose to do.

Walking—It's best to walk primarily on a level, soft surface. Though if you're a hiker, great! But don't think you have to start out walking up hills. A nice walk through your neighborhood is fine. Hey, people even walk through indoor malls at a regular pace for a certain amount of time to get their exercise, which is great for those of you who live in places with cold winters. (See, there are no excuses!)

You may want to consider purchasing a step-o-meter or pedometer—you wear it and it measures how many steps you're taking every day. That's really useful because then you can gauge how much you're walking, even just doing chores or shopping. The American Podiatric Medical Association says that walking one mile is about 2,000 average steps. Walking a block is about 200 average steps. Bicycling or swimming equals 150 steps for each minute. Roller-skating is about 200 steps per minute. So, if you do one of these exercises for twenty minutes, you can figure out the equivalent in steps.

Swimming—Swimming is a non-weight-bearing exercise, but it still serves as a form of resistance training. So, you're not wearing out your joints, but you are getting an amazing cardiovascular workout and building muscle tone and strength.

Stationary bike—I like stationary bikes because they give you a cardiovascular workout. You sweat, but you're not pounding on your joints. And they're small enough to have in your home, which makes it a very convenient way to exercise.

Running—Many people really like running and many hate it! Don't force yourself to run if you don't want to; it can cause harm if it isn't done right, so find something else to do. However, if you do run, know that you are pounding the surface and carefully choose where you run. For instance, run on a track or run in the park rather than on hard pavement. Make sure you have the proper shoes—good-quality running shoes—to help absorb the shock. Many people who run get into a running routine. In other words, you like the neighborhood, so you start at a particular spot and go around the neighborhood a certain way and then arrive back home. What I'd ask you to do is to change the route occasionally. One, so you don't get bored with it. Two, if you run the same route, you're going to be striking the same slopes and curves every time you hit them. If you vary that by going the opposite way instead, for example, you can create better balance in your body and prevent an imbalance from developing.

Weight lifting—I'm in favor of lifting weights only to the point of improving muscle tone. The best way to do this is by not using a lot of weight. Use a lower amount of weight, but do the lifts with more repetitions (reps). That way you build tone and strength without hurting yourself. If you're a bodybuilder type, that's a different matter and you're probably working with a trainer to advise you. However, for exercising the body and keeping fit, low weights and high reps are the best.

With the popularity of the computer, the Internet, and bigger and better TVs, we're just not moving like we used to. It really is becoming a serious health challenge that's showing up in increasing obesity rates and related health problems. Remember, the new government guidelines suggest exercising one hour or more each day most days of the week. The good news is it's not necessary to exercise one hour at a time. Try thirty minutes in the morning and thirty minutes in the evening. Or you could exercise for short periods throughout the day— at breakfast time, lunchtime, and dinnertime. Just get moving—it is absolutely critical for your well-being and overall health. So exercise!

CHAPTER 8

Habit Number Five:
Eat Right

WHY DO YOU NEED TO EAT RIGHT? TO LIVE! The *San Diego Union-Tribune* reported the findings of a recent study: "One in every five cancer deaths in women and one in every seven in men are due to excess pounds. The study by the American Cancer Society is by far the largest . . . more than 900,000 people were followed for sixteen years."[1] There it is in black and white, based on science and research. If you eat too much and end up with too many pounds on your body, you are at a higher risk of dying from cancer. You shouldn't need to read another word to convince you to go from eating whatever you want, whenever you want, to eating right.

We Americans are supersizing ourselves to death. It's gotten to be a big deal (pun intended). Obesity is literally killing us. According to the National Center for Chronic Disease Prevention and Health Promotion, poor diet, physical inactivity, and obesity killed 400,000 people in 2000 and will become the number-one killers of Americans by the end of 2005. Based on this trend, overeating will be more dangerous than smoking because it will kill more people. That's how far out of whack we are!

That's why you have to eat right. Later in this chapter, I'm going to go into detail about the kind of foods I call superfoods. At this point, I want you to commit to making it a habit—eat right. You can do it.

WHAT'S IN IT, ANYWAY?

know what's in the food you put inside your body? Not really,
's a little trick you play on yourself to avoid thinking about
quences of your choices. Well, I'm going to ask you to stop
just grabbing whatever comes your way because it's on a
ead think about what's in it.

If you were to come to my house for dinner, I'd be standing in the kitchen preparing the food with my own hands. If you came over to me and said, "Hey, Andy, what are you making? What's in it?" I'd tell you exactly what I'm making. However, when you go out to dinner to a place you've never been before, where they don't know your name, and you sit at a strange table with a strange waiter and order off the menu, you don't even ask what's in the food.

What *is* in it, anyway? When you come to my house, I'm going to make sure what I serve is healthy. I'll feed you with good food and good-quality products, and so will anyone else you know who cares about you. Go ahead and ask me, "What's in it?" I love the question—I want to tell you and it doesn't bother me at all. What bothers me is that you'll go to a strange restaurant and won't ask them, "What's in it?" Stop and Think about this.

I want you to understand that it's okay to ask people, "Hey, what's in it? What's this thing made of?" If you don't ask that question, who's going to ask it for you? What if it's something that's harmful to you? Just because most restaurants don't list their ingredients on the menu doesn't mean you don't have the right to know what's in the food. You're not only paying for it, you're putting it into your digestive system. And you're out to have a good time too! Why wouldn't you have the right to ask?

Would you order a dish called "Fettucine XYZ" just because it's on the menu? What if they called it "Fettucine with two eggs, a stick of butter, and a quarter pound of cheese that's sure to clog your arteries if you keep eating it"? That would make you Stop and Think!

OUT-OF-CONTROL PORTION SIZES

This brings me to something else very interesting about food choices—portion size. Portion size has gotten out of control. Nowadays, you go to a restaurant and they bring you more food than you and your family together can ever handle in one meal. Pay attention to portions when you go out to dinner.

When my family goes to a little Italian restaurant we like, we order one pasta dish for three of us—me, my wife, and my daughter, Christina. And we still have leftovers! The restaurant staff asks us, "Gee, is something wrong? Don't you like the food?" We say, "We like it. We just can't eat all this food." They look at us, shake their heads, and say, "You're small eaters." That's what it looks like to them. But to me it looks like we're healthy eaters, we're reasonable eaters.

Then I look over to the next table and see one person eating the same pasta dish, the entire pasta dish. That's along with an appetizer, a salad, dessert, and a cup of coffee. I find that absolutely amazing. I'm wondering if I should start thinking about how to perform CPR or if this person will be able to get up from the table.

Portion size has become a big concern nationally. Now when you go out to dinner, you think, "Wow! That's how much I should be eating!" So, you've added another message that's negative for your health— that huge portions are the norm. You then go home and start thinking, "That's what I should be eating here too."

That relates to another very important issue—increased caloric intake is the reason why people are gaining weight. I read an article in *Eating Well* magazine comparing how orders of french fries have changed over the years. In 1970, when you ordered a bag of regular french fries, they weighed 1.3 ounces and had 110 calories. In 1980, one order of french fries weighed 3.3 ounces and had 330 calories. In 1990, one order of regular french fries weighed 6.6 ounces and had 660 calories.

And the trend just continues today. You did not change your ordering habits. What happened was the portion size changed. Again, you were taught to eat everything on your plate because you're not supposed to waste anything, because there are people starving in the world. So you've got a guilt trip to deal with too. Stop and Think about this one fact: you still eat just one order of french fries, but it is now three times the size it used to be!

I want to give you another example of how portion size plays out. I recently went to a restaurant with my family, and my father-in-law ordered a club soda. The waitress brought a massive glass of club soda to him, a seventy-four-year-old man. He called the waitress over and, in his Sicilian accent, said, "What is this?" The waitress answered, "I thought you ordered a club soda." He said, "Whoa, you expect me to drink all of that? I can't drink that in four days!"

I didn't need to give him a lecture about portion size. He could see for himself that this was way too much club soda. And, of course, throughout the meal I paid attention to how much he actually drank.

He consumed less than 25 percent of that glass of club soda. He couldn't possibly drink it all, but leaving over 75 percent of his order makes him feel guilty. This man comes from Sicily, post–World War II, a place where people lived with starvation and hard times, where they didn't want to waste things.

So, what do you do when you're out at a restaurant and you get a massive portion size of food or drink and you think you're supposed to consume it all? If you leave some of it, then feel guilty about wasting food! What I'm going to tell you right now is this: ask for the small size. Tell the waiter, "I don't want a large order or the big glass. I'm watching my portion size. Just give me good-quality food, good-quality drinks, in the small size."

There's a really good reason to watch your portion size. A study came out recently about how to live longer and it shows you it's really quite simple: if you eat less, you'll live longer and be healthier. Researchers at Washington University in St. Louis studied a group of dieters on a low-calorie, high-nutrition eating plan and found that by carefully controlling calories, there were substantial reductions in risk factors for heart disease. The dieters had been on calorie-restrictive diets for an average of six years. Their daily calorie intake ranged from 1,112 to 1,958 (the typical American diet is 1,976 to 3,537 calories per day), and they generally avoided refined starches and processed foods.[2]

> There's a really good reason to watch your portion size. A study came out recently about how to live longer and it shows you it's really quite simple: if you eat less, you'll live longer and be healthier.

And now I want to show you an example in one person's life. Ben, age seventy-two, started restricting his calorie consumption ten years ago and has been eating 1,400 to 1,500 calories per day since then. At that level, he said he doesn't lose or gain weight. I find it very interesting that by eating 1,500 calories or less per day, this man maintains his normal metabolic rate at a level plateau, and at age seventy-two. Think about this—the typical American diet is somewhere between 2,000 and nearly 3,600 calories a day, in many cases more than double what Ben is eating.

The bottom line—you can eat almost anything you like as long as you decrease your portion size and eat within reason. In other words, do what makes sense. Watch and pay attention to what it is you're putting down your throat. You will lose weight and then be able to maintain your normal weight. And you'll be healthy.

THE SWEET-TOOTH EFFECT

Sugar is destroying the human population. Sugar is in everything, more now than ever before. What's the result? The consumption of sugar has gone up dramatically. In 1922, the average American consumed about 5 pounds of sugar annually. By 1999, Americans consumed an average of 158 pounds of sweeteners, including sugar, high-fructose corn syrup, and honey. And that number has jumped almost 30 percent in just the last twenty years![3]

I had the opportunity to teach a nutrition course at a school for homeless children in San Diego recently. I demonstrated to the kids how sugar adds up throughout the day in their bodies, and I want to show you too.

Look at the back of a regular applesauce container and read the ingredients. It will tell you that there's 22 grams of sugar in the applesauce. The label of a typical candy bar shows that it contains 32 grams of sugar. A soda has an average of 39–50 grams of sugar. Peaches in heavy syrup contain 22 grams of sugar. Even a can of soup has 22 grams of sugar! This is per serving, I might add. Sometimes there's two or more servings in a can. So, if you have the whole can, you double the amount of sugar.

Sugar is destroying the human population. In 1922, the average American consumed about 5 pounds of sugar annually. By 1999, Americans consumed an average of 158 pounds of sweeteners, including sugar, high-fructose corn syrup, and honey.

So, I took a scale that measures in grams. (You might want to do this at home if you have one of these little scales.) I put a cup on the scale. From a bag of sugar, I scooped out 22 grams of sugar for the applesauce. I added the 32 grams of sugar for the candy bar. I scooped out 39 grams more for the soda and 22 grams for the peaches. I threw in the 22 grams for the can of soup. You can see with your own eyes—the entire cup of sugar is overflowing! Look how much sugar a person's eating in just one day. I didn't even have to add all the rest of the sugar you normally take in from pie, cookies, brownies, and bubblegum. Nothing else, and it was already overflowing! That is the sweet-tooth effect.

Now, here's another part of the experiment—use the same types of food, but make some substitutions. Take regular, natural, unsweetened apple sauce and instead of 22 grams of sugar, it drops to 11 grams. Instead of peaches in heavy syrup, replace it with light syrup and you go from 22 grams to 11 grams of sugar. Take the cream of mushroom soup and change it to golden mushroom soup and, again, you cut the sugar in half. Skip the soda and the candy bar.

Now look at that cup of sugar: right away, you'll notice we went from one full cup of refined sugar a day to one-quarter cup of sugar a day. Put in similar healthy foods and you get 75 percent less sugar! You make this big change just by watching the ingredient content.

Why bother with all this? I'll give you one really good reason: diabetes is now out of control. Adult-onset diabetes, an acquired disease, used to be called *adult* for a reason—it was normally seen in individuals older than fifty. However, it's changed. We've started to see more of it in forty-year-olds. In thirty-year-olds, it went up by over 60 percent. We now see it in people in their twenties and teens, even as young as eight years old. Instead of calling it adult-onset diabetes, you'll now hear it referred to as "type II" diabetes. It's not just for adults anymore; it's for kids too! Who would ever want to wish diabetes on their kids? Yet, here we are, shoveling sugar in by the spoonful.

Diabetes is a devastating disease. Many people think, "Oh, well, it can be medically managed. No big deal." Actually, it is quite a big deal. It is the number-one cause of blindness and of amputations. It also causes neurological disorders, cardiovascular disease, and it shortens your life span. And this disease for the most part is an acquired condition. It is *something we do to ourselves* because we're not careful about what we're eating and about our lifestyle.

Just think about soda for a minute. A recent article in the *San Diego Union-Tribune* said, "Despite warnings that soda can contribute to obesity, tooth decay, lack of calcium and type II diabetes, teenagers are drinking it at record numbers."[4] Okay, let's Stop and Think here. Kids think soda is sugary, bubbly, and wonderful. You can drink it with chips, fries, cheeseburgers, even a scoop of ice cream! One kid has five a day— 11 A.M., lunch, after school, 4 P.M. snack, and finally one with dinner.

An average teenager drinks two cans of soda a day, or more than 700 cans a year. Here's one reason they end up doing this. In the mid-1990s, sodas made up 11 percent of the beverages sold at schools, according to the U.S. Department of Agriculture. However, in the mid-1980s, it was less than 3 percent. There's almost four times more soda being sold in schools now! From 1965 to 1996, soft-drink consumption increased by 287 percent in boys and 224 percent in girls. Do you still wonder how that happened? You can just go to the school cafeteria to see why!

As a parent, as a friend, for yourself, wherever you are—whether in an office setting or at a party—what should you do when you find yourself drinking soda pop, having doughnuts, cupcakes, pies, and leftover desserts? Stop and Think. Know that it is all sugar entering your body. Know that it is hurting your vascular system, your pancreas is going crazy, and it can hurt your vision and your nerves. People get diabetic neuropathies that are incredibly painful to extremities, the feet and hands. You feel numbness, tingling, burning—people lose limbs.

These days, low-carbohydrate diets have hit the market and everyone's talking about them and trying them. There are books and diet methods galore. No matter which method you try, decreasing your carbohydrates means decreasing your total caloric intake. Of course, carbohydrates break down into simple sugars, so you're decreasing your overall sugar intake.

Experts from everywhere are telling you the same things and you need to listen. There's a global epidemic in obesity-related diseases, including heart disease, diabetes, and cancer, and poor diet is a major factor. That's according to a recent study from the World Health Organization and the Food and Agricultural Organization. Experts from around the world compiled the data. To combat obesity, they recommend regular exercise and a diet low in fats (15 to 30 percent of calories), salt (less than 5 grams daily), and sugar (less than 10 percent of calories).[5] This sugar recommendation is more specific than the United States government's dietary guidelines, which simply say that sugar should be used in moderation. Well, guess what, that's not working!

How can you avoid being too sweet? If you're going to take in less than 10 percent of your daily calories from sugar, that means, out of a 2,000-calories-a-day diet, sugar should be no more than 200 calories or 50 grams (each gram of sugar equals 4 calories). For clues to see if sugar's been added to a food, look at the ingredients. Start reading the ingredients label on the cans and food products you're eating. And it'll say sugar in some form or other—white, brown, raw, or cane; corn syrup or high-fructose corn syrup; honey; molasses or sorghum syrup; fruit-juice concentrate. The first ingredients listed on the label are the ones in the product at the highest concentrations. So, if corn syrup or sugar is the first or second ingredient, that means there's a lot of it. Labels will also usually list the actual grams of sugars or carbohydrates in the nutrition information.

Sure, sugar is fun and it tastes good. But what's the cost? What is it doing to your health? How is it going to affect your longevity and vitality? Stop and Think about it.

MAKING CHANGES

You need to eat five servings of fruits and vegetables a day. That's ten in all—five fruits and five vegetables. But a lot of people still don't do it. Well, it's time to act on it.

There's someone who works in my clinic who's an insulin-dependent diabetic. So, what do I do? As an employer, I don't harp on my staff. I don't ask where they eat or how they eat. Their personal lives are their own business, even though I'd really like them to live healthily.

My wife, Sallie, works at the office three days a week. My wife is also a health nut. She sees this member of the staff go across the street to McDonald's every day, and she says, "What's going on? You eat fast food five nights a week, you eat fast food for breakfast every day. You can't do this. Do you eat vegetables?"

Staff member: I don't even have a vegetable in the house.

Sallie: You're a diabetic? You're thirty-two years old and a diabetic. You need to change your diet.

Staff member: How do you do that? Like, how do you make an artichoke?

Sallie: Put it in boiling water for five minutes.

Then my wife goes on to describe how to do other simple recipes with vegetables. The staff member tries it. Her blood sugar gradually returns to normal and she gets off insulin. Why? She changed her diet and she hasn't been out to dinner except for her husband's birthday. That was a lifesaver. People need to make changes if they want to get and stay healthy.

What's the other side of eating right? I'll tell you. My friend John comes into the office one day.

Doc Andy: Hey, John, how are you doing?

John: I don't feel good.

Doc Andy: Yes, I know, but what's wrong with you?

John: Andy, if I knew what was wrong with me, why would I come to see you? I don't feel good. I turned forty and I've been going downhill ever since.

So I go through his paperwork and see he has frequent urination. He's forty years old, which is kind of young for a prostate problem. Does he have a kidney problem? Is he diabetic? Then it pops out that he has more than five caffeine drinks a day.

Doc Andy: Listen, in your papers you marked off that you drink more than five caffeinated drinks a day.

John: I drink coffee.

Doc Andy: Well, how many cups a day do you drink? Like five or six cups a day?

John: No, I drink thirty.

Doc Andy: Thirty! Are you sure—*thirty?*

John: Yeah, about five or six pots a day.

Doc Andy: Are you out of your mind? Of course you have frequent urination!

Here's what John does. He drives a delivery truck twelve hours a day and he drinks coffee all the time. Thirty cups a day! How many cups is that in a week? Two hundred and ten. How many cups in a month? Almost 900 cups of coffee a month! It's no wonder he doesn't feel well.

One of my patients works for a well-known coffee house. So, I asked him one day, "Tell me, how often does the same person come back in a day? Twice? Three times?"

He replies, "Oh, we have people who come back several times a day."

It goes like this: they come in first thing in the morning for a triple espresso. Then, it's back at 10 o'clock for their mid-morning coffee break, then lunch time, 3 P.M., and 5 P.M. for the drive home. And so it goes on and on. How can they afford so many cups of coffee?

Have you seen how these places make their coffee? They spin it around, slap some cream on it, pour some foam in, sprinkle some sugary stuff on top . . . it doesn't even look like a cup of coffee!

Patients tell me, "I drink just one coffee a day. And, oh yeah, I drink a soda a day." More caffeine. "And then I drink one martini a day too. And, of course, I have to have my Snickers bar." Anything else? "Yeah, I

like Jell-O cups—just one of those. And I only get one order of fries."
Anything else? "Sure, I smoke one cigar a day."

Notice something here? As I mentioned earlier, one of everything
became twenty bad things in one day. And, by the way, eating right
means drinking right. Coffee isn't going to give you any nutrition, and
drinking a lot of coffee is even worse. You aren't just eating one bad
thing a day or drinking one bad drink a day. You're eating and drinking
one plus one plus one plus one . . . and on and on. So, turn that habit
around. Eat one apple plus one banana plus one handful of walnuts
plus one avocado instead.

You may not notice right away the effects your bad eating and
drinking habits are having on your body. Because your body is a
supreme being, it's built so well that it can withstand a lot of abuse. But
eventually it catches up. I'm helping you to stop it from deteriorating
right now. Eat right.

ADD COLOR TO YOUR DIET

The more color you have in your diet with respect to fruits and vegetables, the healthier your diet will be and the healthier you will be
as a result. Add a variety of foods, combining colors, because they all
have strengths and weaknesses.

> The more
> color you have in
> your diet with respect to
> fruits and vegetables, the
> healthier your diet will
> be and the healthier
> you will be as
> a result.

I want you to understand the
science behind the choices you
make. In the June 2001 issue of
Environmental Nutrition, there's
a very good description of food
colors and why foods that have
those colors are good for you.
Because I think this is an easy
way to introduce you to healthy
foods to put in your bowls (see
"Bowls and More Bowls" on page 77),
I'll identify some of those the foods by
their colors and list their key nutrients.[6]

Red—Red fruits and vegetables are critical because they contain the
phytonutrient lycopene, which is a carotenoid and antioxidant that

Bowls and More Bowls

One of the major obstacles we have in life is the temptation to snack. Snacking creates many of the health challenges we have today. Most people snack on fast food, candy, gum, cookies, sugary foods, fat foods, artificial colors and dyes, and other synthetic foods. The way to fight this off, the way to be successful, is to set out the bowls.

Right this moment, today, I want you to take eight to twelve bowls and place them all over your home. In those bowls, put live foods, healthy foods—for instance, grapes, cherries, apples, oranges, nuts, seeds, trail mix, raisins, and dried fruits. Put them everywhere. In fact, I want you to get together with your family and pick the foods together—decide what you are going to have and what your kids like. Make the trail mix yourself and put it out there.

Then, get rid of the other foods—the cookies, chips, pies, candy bars, and sodas. All of those things must go. When you get home and you're hungry, you want to snack on something right away. So, what do you do? Reach for the bowls. Put them in front of you: make it easy and accessible. Set yourself up to win. When you do that, you'll be snacking, but you'll be snacking on food that is healthy for you.

Otherwise, snacking causes a whole lot of trouble. It's taking you over the top. You're adding those extra calories, and it's putting on 10, 20, or more pounds a year.

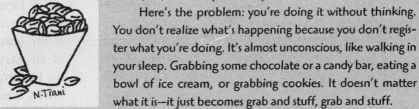

Here's the problem: you're doing it without thinking. You don't realize what's happening because you don't register what you're doing. It's almost unconscious, like walking in your sleep. Grabbing some chocolate or a candy bar, eating a bowl of ice cream, or grabbing cookies. It doesn't matter what it is—it just becomes grab and stuff, grab and stuff.

Stop and Think about what you're doing and what you're putting in your mouth. Why not grab raspberries, cranberries, apples, oranges, grapes, cherries, bananas, chopped-up cucumbers, carrots, seeds, or nuts? Those choices are far better. What you need to do is set up the bowls. Stop sabotaging your home and set yourself up to win.

may protect against prostate and other cancers. Sources of lycopene include pink grapefruit, tomatoes and tomato sauce, and watermelon.

Red-purple—These foods contain anthocyanins, which are great antioxidants. Red-purple foods include blackberries, blueberries, cherries, grapes, prunes, strawberries, red apples, and red bell peppers. Those are some of the red and purple fruits and vegetables you can add to your bowls of healthy snacks. Eggplant is also in this category. You can steam, bake, or boil eggplant, then peel and mash it; add some seasoning, some lemon, and dip carrots or celery sticks into it.

Orange-yellow—Orange-yellow foods contain alpha- and beta-carotene, carotenoids, and limonoids, which can help prevent cancer. Sources include apricots, nectarines, cantaloupes, carrots, mangoes, oranges, peaches, pineapples, squash, sweet potatoes, and tangerines.

Green-yellow—Green and yellow foods contain sulforaphane, indoles, lutein, zeaxanthin, and carotenoids. Foods include avocados, bok choy, broccoli, Brussels sprouts, cabbage, cauliflower, cucumbers, green beans, kale, kiwi, spinach, and zucchini. There are plenty of choices, so if you don't like one, you'll like another. Be willing to try something you've never eaten before.

White-green—These foods contain allicin and flavonoids. Good food sources include asparagus, celery, endive, garlic, leeks, mushrooms, and onions.

So, color up your home, color up your kitchen, color up your diet, and you're going to color up the inside of your body. You can make it easy on yourself. Bowls and colors—that's all you need to get you started.

H_2O IS ALL YOU NEED TO KNOW

Let's picture a beautiful plant: green, shiny, vibrant, blossoming with flowers. It's beautiful, absolutely the best that nature can produce. Now, if we deprive that plant of water (H_2O), what happens to it? Within days, it begins to wither, the leaves start to bend over, crunch in, drop off the branches, and change color. We can tell visually that the plant is suffering.

N.Trani

What do you think is happening to the 75 trillion cells in your body when they don't have enough water? They are also withering, crunching, starving, and dying. Water is the key to life for all living things on Earth. In your body, your supreme being, you need water.

When you don't have enough water, you feel depressed and lethargic, a lack of energy. And what's the first thing you probably do? You run off to the nearest coffee place. "I need coffee. I need caffeine." Or you go to the convenience store. "I need a candy bar. I need a soda pop." Or maybe you even head to the medicine cabinet. "I need Prozac. I need Zoloft."

What you really need is water. Stop and Think about this. When you need energy, what your body is really lacking is water. Without water, the body doesn't survive. You need to drink at least eight to twelve 8-ounce glasses per day. Are you doing that? A cup of coffee or a cup of tea does not equal water. You need pure water in your body to help clear out your kidneys, clean out your body, oxygenate yourself, and give yourself life. By not drinking enough water, you are missing out on one of the most fundamental ways to have a healthy lifestyle.

I recently attended a seminar where one of the speakers, a doctor, said he felt that water should be considered a food, which I found very interesting. How long would your body survive without water? The answer is about one and a half to two and a half weeks. That would be it. How long could you survive without food? About six weeks. So, water is absolutely necessary to life, but we usually talk more about the importance of food instead of focusing on how critical water is.

Here's a simple quiz: What has no calories, no vitamins, no fat, and no sugar, but without it we can't survive? Water! Even without any of these nutrients in it, water is still essential for all living things. What is the most common substance on Earth? Water! It's all around us, it's available, it's even free. But are we putting the right amount of it into our bodies? There are no excuses here.

Nearly 75 percent of adult body weight is water—that's about 10–12 gallons. In other words, it's the most important substance in the body. Water helps maintain all the organs in the body and is important for regulating body temperature. Without water, your body couldn't absorb foods and nutrients and move them throughout the body. Drinking plenty of water can help reduce the pain of arthritis, lower-back problems, and migraines. There's even evidence it can lower high cholesterol and high blood pressure.[7]

We actually lose a pint or more of water every day just from breathing. Dehydration can lead to a number of problems and symptoms, including headaches, dizziness, cramps, loss of muscle strength, and, in severe cases, heat exhaustion and heatstroke.[8]

Water is low in sodium and has no fat, and it is readily absorbed by the body instead of flowing straight through like coffee or other liquids, which also often flush out nutrients with them. Caffeine and alcohol are actually diuretics; that is, they stimulate the body to lose water! Your body needs a certain amount of fluids each day and water is the best choice. What more do you need to know to convince yourself to drink water instead of caffeine, artificial flavors and sweeteners, and sugar?

So, as I said earlier, you need eight to twelve 8-ounce glasses of water per day for optimum health. Of course, this may vary depending on your body size and activity levels. Here's a simple way to calculate how much water you might need: weigh yourself and divide your weight in pounds by half; that number in ounces is how much water you should be drinking daily. If you weigh 128 pounds, divide that by two and you get 64. So, each day you should try to drink 64 ounces of water or eight 8-ounce glasses.[9]

If you exercise, you'll need to drink more water to maintain proper hydration. Drink water before you start exercising, about every twenty minutes while exercising, and after you finish too. You should do this whether or not you feel thirsty, because thirst is not always an accurate indicator of water needs while exercising. You may also need more water if you are pregnant, a nursing mother, elderly, or dieting.[10]

You need to Stop and Think about water more than ever. It used to be that people didn't have all these other choices of drinks and so they drank water, but now sodas and coffees and fruit-flavored drinks are flying off the shelves. And this trend toward drinking sugar and caffeine comes at a time when our active lifestyles call for more water than ever. People are dieting, taking prescription and over-the-counter drugs, spending hours per day in dry air-conditioned buildings, traveling on airplanes where the air is almost completely without moisture—all of these things dehydrate the body.

If you don't replenish that water, what happens? You get symptoms—migraine headaches, feeling weak and tired, perhaps nausea. So you take an Advil, a pep pill, a headache pill, or a stomach pill. Are you solving the problem? No, you're compounding it, because medications just make you more dehydrated. They are not the solution.

What is the solution? Water. Water is life. H_2O is all you need to know. Drinking water is as close to using the bounty of nature as you can get.

NATURAL FOODS—THE CLOSER, THE BETTER

Fruits and vegetables are good for you—plain, simple, straightforward, and true. I've never read a study that said they were bad for you.

But what happens when you actually eat them? This is what I hear: "Dr. Andy, I can't eat vegetables plain. I've got to put something on them so they taste better." So you throw on some butter, then shake some salt over the whole thing. What you're doing is getting further away from natural food, adding ingredients that are a little bit worse for your health—more salt, more fat.

Butter's bad enough, but then several years ago you heard a new message from the manufacturers of chemical food: margarine is better. Now you've gone another step further away from natural food—from plain vegetable to butter and salt to margarine. It's a little bit worse for you than before. Just keep that thought in your mind.

Let's talk about going out to dinner. You go to the fanciest and best restaurant in town. What do you have first? A cocktail. Then what? Some bread—maybe sourdough bread with butter. Then you have a salad, with extra blue cheese dressing, an entrée, dessert, and a cup of coffee. Then you grab a pink or blue packet of chemical sugar substitute and pour it in your coffee.

As I imagine this, I'm thinking, "What, are you kidding me? Now you're worried about the calories? When you get to the coffee you decide to do something about how many calories you're taking in? And what do you decide to do? Add an artificial chemical!" Listen, the further you get away from a natural food, the worse it is for you. Artificial sweeteners, artificial colors, artificial dyes—those things hurt you. Stop and Think about that.

Here's an example of a discussion I have with patients who ask me about adding to a natural food:

"Well, Doc Andy. What about a piece of corn?"

Here's my answer: "Okay, let's talk about a piece of corn. Let's say we go out to the farm, grab a piece of corn, wash it off, and eat it just like that. Naturally, raw."

And they say, "I don't want it that way."

"Well, how would you like it?"

"I like mine steamed."

Okay, so let's steam that corn.

And another person comes up and says, "No, I don't like it that way."
"Well, how do you like it?"
"I like mine boiled."
"Oh, okay, so you want yours boiled." So, let's boil it.
And another person says, "No, I don't like it that way. I like mine barbequed."
"Okay, so let's barbeque it."
Another says to me, "No, I don't like it that way. I like mine canned."
We're still talking about that piece of corn, but look how different it becomes. Right from the vine, we've mashed it, smashed it, cooked it, boiled it, barbecued it, even nuked it. We've done everything to it. It's still a piece of corn, but remember this—the further you get away from its natural state, the more you ruin it. In other words, the more you destroy it, the more you alter its normal chemistry, the less value it's going to have for you nutritionally. So, you want to keep your vegetables as fresh and as close to the vine as possible for maximum nutrition and benefit.

When I bring up the importance of eating as many fruits and vegetables as possible, a lot of people ask me, "What about pesticides?" Look, pesticides are not a problem caused by the vegetables—they're a problem caused by the humans who add them and end up sabotaging fruits and vegetables. Wash your produce thoroughly, buy organic if you can, but don't use pesticides as an excuse not to eat them! Eat your fruits and vegetables and eat them in their most natural state.

SUPERFOOD IS SUPER FOR YOU

I'm going to give you enough information so that you begin to see which foods are beneficial to you and what you should be feeding your body. Why do you need to know this? Here's a headline that should make you sit up and pay attention: "THE WAY WE EAT IS MAKING US SICK." That's right. *The way we eat is making us sick.* According to the World Health Organization in Geneva, more people are becoming sick because their eating habits are changing to favor prepared foods from supermarkets or take-out foods from restaurants instead of self-prepared meals.

Doctors worldwide are finding an increase in bacteria and food-borne infections. It's not just a stomachache they're talking about, but infectious diseases like salmonella and *E. coli,* which can have ex-

tremely serious consequences like bloody diarrhea and even loss of
a pregnancy. These diseases can kill you. Why is this happening? People don't take the time to cook food as much as they used to. The increased use of prepared foods means we're eating on the run more.
So, we're eating on the run and we're running ourselves right into the
grave. Don't keep running to the takeout line, the fast-food restaurant,
the pretty package in the grocery store. Stop and Think.

It is extremely important that you feed your body good, nutritious
food all the time. Don't continue to eat fast food, prepared food, glow-
in-the-dark food. Eat superfoods. What are superfoods? I'm going to
list a few of them in alphabetical order, so there's no real order of pref-
erence. They all have their strengths. I don't have every good food
listed here, but I want to show you the advantages of some key foods
that you can easily prepare in your home every day.

You should try to have a variety of nutritious foods in your diet. The
reason is that not all foods have the same benefits. The body requires
all of the nutrients, including vitamins, minerals, and phytochemicals,
it can get. It needs as many antioxidant-rich foods as possible to fight
against free-radical damage, which helps prevent stroke, cardiovascular disease, degenerative disorders, and cancer. All foods that I mention
on the following pages have benefits for your body, and you should put
a variety of them in your daily diet. Don't just pick out the one or two
foods you're familiar with and you're sure you like. Get a wide spectrum

of foods because all of them have different strengths and weaknesses.

Now, in some of my examples, I'm going to use the scientific names for their ingredients. Look, I can't always pronounce or remember those words easily, and you don't need to memorize them either. What you do need to do is recognize that foods like blueberries and broccoli may just look like pretty plants, but they pack dynamite chemicals for your health. These days, we've gotten so used to looking at cardboard packages made by the manufacturers of prepared foods that we've forgotten how really good the ingredients are on their own, and how they come directly from nature. I'm also going to refer to scientific studies, because the research is also telling you these blueberries or avocados or lentils are good for you. There's proof.

Did anyone ever tell you that a box of pre-cooked, pre-packaged food is good for you because it's in a bright carton with a cartoon character on it telling you to buy it and have fun? No way. You've got to get beyond the hype and the packaging to find the foods that really help you live well. I've pulled together some of the top foods from the studies I've read. At the end of this chapter, there is a resource list of magazines and newsletters that you might want to start reading too. There's new information on healthy foods coming out every day! Make your own list of favorites and pick up those healthy foods whenever you go shopping, and pass right by the junk food.

Asparagus—Here's a common vegetable that has a lot of good nutrients. Asparagus is high in folate and the other B vitamins. Why would you care? Because folate and the other B vitamins can help reduce the risk of colon and cervical cancer. Folate may delay the onset of cancer by preventing DNA damage. Other foods that are high in folate are orange juice, lentils, beans, spinach, peanuts, and broccoli. Every day of the week you could be eating something different that's high in folate and help protect yourself against the risk of cancer.

Avocados—Avocados contain more blood-pressure-lowering potassium than bananas. Potassium protects against strokes: people who don't get enough potassium in their diets, or who are taking diuretics and have low blood levels of potassium, may be at a higher risk of stroke. I know I don't have to ask you which you'd rather do, go to the hospital with a stroke or eat avocados.

What makes avocados so good is that they are rich in unsaturated fats. They also contain phytonutrients that help provide cholesterol-lowering beta-sitosterol and cancer-protective glutathione, along with vitamin E, folate, vitamin B_6, and fiber. Each avocado has about 300 calories—if you eat a lot of avocados, you're going to have health benefits, but you also need to be careful about the calories. Nature has its checks and balances, and you can end up with too much of a good thing. That's why you always need to Stop and Think. Am I eating any avocados? Enough avocados or too many?

Berries—I'm a real fan of berries. They have high-potency antioxidants that fight against free-radical damage, and they help oxygenate the brain and the blood. You should make berries an everyday part of your diet: choose among blueberries, blackberries, cranberries, raspberries, and strawberries. Take blueberries, for example. They have anthocyanin, the pigment that gives them their special blue color, which is a powerful antioxidant. Blueberries also contain 4 grams of fiber per cup, a good dose of vitamin C, ellagic acid to help protect against cancer, and tannins that help prevent urinary tract infections. Plus, they boost brain health and vision. They even look great and taste sweet. Why reach for a cookie when you can get the "power of blue" or red or black? Eat a half cup of berries a day, every day. If you can't get fresh ones, get frozen ones, but put them in your diet.

Brazil nuts—You'd have to be nuts not to eat nuts. Brazil nuts are loaded with selenium, a promising anticancer nutrient. Research suggests that 300 micrograms (mcg) of selenium a day may reduce the risk of prostate, colon, and lung cancers. Selenium is a powerful antioxidant that may bolster apoptosis, which means suicide of the cancer cells. A cautionary note about Brazil nuts: toxicity can occur if you eat more than 800 mcg a day. One large or two medium nuts in the shell contain less than 200 mcg, so be careful not to exceed the toxic level. It's that balance in nature—you shouldn't go overboard and stuff yourself.

Broccoli—You bypass broccoli and you miss out on sulforaphane, indole-3-carbinol, and isothiocyanates, which are potent anticancer substances. Researchers are finding that these substances modify estrogen so that it's less damaging, and they increase the activity of enzymes that defuse carcinogens. Now that you know this, what should you do? Eat three servings of broccoli a week. Or add some variety and eat broccoli's cousins too: bok choy, Brussels sprouts, cauliflower, kale, and cabbage.

A few years ago, it came out that the first President Bush didn't like broccoli. It became a big news story causing a lot of controversy. I don't want you to say, "I don't like broccoli or cabbage or kale." They're really good for you, and you can find lots of tasty ways to cook them so you can protect yourself against cancer.

Fish—Cold-water fish such as salmon, sardines, bluefish, mackerel, and tuna are loaded with omega-3 fatty acids. Studies have found that people who eat fish just twice a week have a 30 to 50 percent lower risk of cancers of the mouth, esophagus, stomach, pancreas, colon, and rectum than those who eat fewer than one serving of fish a week. So, the omega-3 fatty acids are important to include in the diet: they help decrease blood clotting, prevent heart arrhythmias, and combat inflammation. These are bonuses for the heart. What if you don't like fish? There's a great plant source of omega-3 fatty acids—flaxseed. Incorporate flaxseeds or flaxseed oil into your diet instead.

Kiwifruit—This is a fruit that's named after a bird, a little New Zealand bird that doesn't fly, and it's a nutritional goldmine. Kiwifruit is one of the most nutrient-dense fruits of all the commonly eaten fruits. Two medium-sized kiwis have more potassium (505 milligrams) than a banana and twice the vitamin C (114 milligrams) of an orange—all for just under 100 calories! Kiwis are also a good source of folate, magnesium, vitamin E, copper, and lutein. That last one, lutein, is a phytonutrient thought to reduce the risk of cancer, heart disease, and macular degeneration, an eye disease that causes reduction in sight, even blindness, in older people. Copper is important for red blood cell formation.

Believe it or not, kiwifruit can also be used as a meat tenderizer because it contains an enzyme called actinidine, which breaks down the meat. But don't marinate your meat in kiwifruit for more than thirty minutes, because it will become too mushy. That tells you just how potent kiwis are.

Lentils—On a personal note, lentils are one of my favorite foods. My wife makes pasta with lentils—my kids enjoy it, I enjoy it, and it's very tasty. The thing I like most about lentils is that not only do they taste terrific, but they're also really healthy for you. They protect the heart with nutrients like folate (179 milligrams per half cup) and fiber (both soluble and insoluble, 8 grams per half cup). If you're a vegetarian or don't like to eat meat, eat lentils instead! They have 9 grams of protein and more than 3 milligrams of iron, which makes them a nutritious meat alternative. Lentils are available in lots of colors too—brown, green, red, orange, and yellow, so they make a good-looking, tasty, nutritious meal. Eat them!

Tomatoes—Tomatoes contain a substance called lycopene. It's what makes the tomatoes red and it's also an antioxidant that protects against several types of cancer, including prostate, lung, and colon cancer. Lycopene also protects against heart disease and bone loss. It turns out that lycopene is better absorbed when the tomatoes are cooked, because cooking breaks the chemical bonds and lets you absorb the nutrients better. So, include tomatoes and tomato sauces in everything—they're good for you!

Watermelon—What should you do if you're at a picnic or sitting by the side of your pool? Grab some watermelon. You've read about how tomatoes are a superfood because they contain cancer-fighting lycopene. Well, watermelon averages about 40 percent more lycopene than tomatoes per serving, and you don't have to cook the watermelon to get the benefits. If you're eating both your tomatoes *and* your watermelon, you're really covering your lycopene.

I've only listed a few foods here. There are many, many more, but I wanted to give you an idea of what's possible and what foods you should consider including in your everyday life. As you can see, there are many reasons why you should eat these superfoods.

Many of the foods I've mentioned are pretty familiar, but you may not have heard about a less familiar superfood—wheat grass, also known as "green gold" or "nature's most complete food." What is wheat grass? It's the grass of green wheat plants that are no more than two weeks old. A single ounce of its juice (a typical serving) is packed with protein, glucose, chlorophyll, enzymes, vitamins A, C, and E, several B vitamins, and vitamin K. It puts many minerals, including calcium, iron, sodium, potassium, magnesium, selenium, and zinc, into your body!

Studies in the United States, Russia, and Japan dating back as far as the 1940s found that wheat grass juice may help heal or prevent some cancers. It can inhibit cancer cell growth, cure skin conditions like acne, repair some types of DNA damage, and ease inflammation. Alternative-medicine experts say it is also a great blood and liver cleanser. Wheat grass juice is becoming much more popular in the United States, in juice bars and at health spas. Try it!

Recommended Publications for Health Information

Nutrition Action Healthletter

Environmental Nutrition

Harvard Health Letter

Tufts University Health and Nutrition Letter

Eating Well Magazine

Life Extension Magazine

Body and Soul Magazine

Health magazine (website: www.health.com)

What Color Is Your Diet by David Heber (Regan Books, 2001)

FINAL THOUGHTS

Open up your horizons when it comes to food choices. Know that there's more out there than just fast foods, french fries, soda pop, and candy bars—all that nonsense that's actually destroying us. There are life-giving foods available that can protect us and make our bodies stronger and healthier. You just have to make the right choices.

Take this book with you to the grocery store for healthier shopping. Remember the "bowls and more bowls" program? You're going to take bowls full of these superfoods and put them around your house, in your office, all over the place. When you're hungry or want a snack, reach for these foods. Reach for asparagus, Brazil nuts, berries, or have a warm bowl of lentil soup.

I want to bring up another point about getting the right amount of nutrition. Sometimes you simply can't get all the nutrients you need from food. The soil has been depleted, the food has been sitting on the supermarket shelf too long, or cooking kills too many of the nutrients. And sometimes, hard as you may try, you don't have available all the healthy foods you need. Maybe you're traveling or working long hours. Life brings a lot of challenges, and I understand that.

> Know that there's more out there than just fast foods, french fries, soda pop, and candy bars—all that nonsense that's actually destroying us. There are life-giving foods available that can protect us and make our bodies stronger and healthier.

That's why it's important to take nutritional supplements. Good vitamin and mineral supplements are made with natural ingredients, are processed and stored so they don't deteriorate, and are then delivered to you in a form that your body can readily absorb. I encourage you to supplement your diet with vitamins, minerals, and antioxidants. A good daily multivitamin and mineral supplement can give you the minimum recommended dietary allowance (RDA) of those nutrients. No matter what hassles life throws your way to keep you from getting to the best foods, you'll know you've got the minimum needed to support your health each day. You may also need to add specific supplements to address particular deficiencies in your body or for illnesses that you are fighting. That's good too. Being flexible about what you need, what works best for you, and how supplements fill the bill is all part of making healthy choices.

CHAPTER 9

Habit Number Six:
Clean Your Mind

WHY SHOULD YOU CLEAN YOUR MIND? Because the nervous system goes all through the body, coordinating and controlling every single cell. If you put your subconscious mind in a poor state, what do you think is going to happen to your body functions? Poor attitude leads to a dysfunctional body. Your conscious mind may be in a poor state too, if you make bad decisions, let yourself eat unhealthy food, or do something that hurts your body. What happens if you sabotage your brain? It's all over.

To put it in plain words: no stinky thinking! Let me give you an example:

Patient: Doc, I eat right. I'm calm when I eat my meal.

Doc Andy: You are?

Patient: I go home. I put on my pajamas. I make a nice a dinner, sit down, and turn on the TV.

Doc Andy: And what's on the TV?

Patient: The six o'clock news, of course.

Negative! Bombs, fires, car crashes—they're all over the news. And how does the nervous system react? It's toasted. That's how you sabotage a good meal and yourself.

I have a rule at my house: no TV while we eat. Now, I'm a big sports fan. I love sports. In fact, I'm a major sports fanatic—football, basketball, baseball, you name it. I have two brothers who also love sports. So, when my family comes to my house for dinner on Sunday, what do I do? I turn off the TV.

"Whoa!" they scream. "What are you doing? The game's on!"

"I know," I tell them, "but we don't watch TV when we're eating at my house."

At their homes, the TV is on when they eat. When I go there, even if I don't want to participate, my ears are hearing it, so then I have to look! But what's on at dinnertime? The news. I don't watch the news, because it's mostly negative. Does this mean I don't care what's going on in the world or my community? Absolutely not. All it means is that I don't need to know while I'm eating. So, how do I get my information? I'm a read-a-holic. I have so many newspapers, they're going to push me out of my office. But when you read, you get to pick and choose what you're putting into your brain. When you turn on the TV, you have no idea what's about to enter into your mind. Keep the bombs and fires away when you digest your food.

Cleaning your mind is not just about keeping away negative words and images; it's also about letting in positive ideas and feelings. Some people call this spiritual sense the universe, Mother Nature, God, life itself. It doesn't matter what you call it or how you worship, the main thing is that you tap into that life force—one of the most powerful tools for a long, healthy life that a person can have.

It happens every time a baby is born, a tree sprouts, clouds pass overhead, rain falls, the ocean's tides go in and out, the mountains stand majestically, the desert sits in heat and stillness—they are all miracles. Just getting up with the sun, walking across the street, or hugging your child is a kind of miracle. Connect with that experience. I believe if there is a deadness inside of you, an emptiness, it's hard to be a whole, healthy person. Don't lose the connectedness: find a place to connect to that greatness and you will find the way to connect to the healthy abundance of being alive.

JUMPING ROPE

Have you ever watched little kids jumping rope? There are generally three or four kids, usually girls, with two of the girls each holding one end of the rope. The rope's going up and down, round and round. The kids are singing a little song. One girl leaps into the moving rope and then jumps up and down. And when she gets tired, she leaps out and another girl jumps in. The rope continues to turn.

So, here's what happens in life: we're born, we play, we go to school, we get out of school and go right to work, we keep going to work, we fall down, we collapse. That's why we need to remember the principles of jumping rope: you jump in, you jump up and down, and then you jump out. That last point is the one we're ignoring. You have to jump out now and then too.

It's thought that up to 80 percent of health problems are stress related. When you go to work, when you're taking care of your family, or when you're helping out your community, you put in so much effort that you feel tired and stressed, and you get angry, forgetful, and distracted. That's the time to jump out! Maybe it means taking a three-day vacation or a half-hour walk, but take a time-out when you need it.

Take a breather, relax, and get yourself together. Get your body in shape and make sure you reestablish your focus and remember what's important. Then, when you're ready, jump back in again.

What happens if you don't take breaks? You get burned out. You start experiencing mental fatigue, you feel unhappy, even depressed, and you are tired all the time. You stop liking your job or you may yell at the kids. You feel like you're stuck. And then you don't make healthy choices. You feel worse because your mind and body aren't getting the nutrients, the water, and the exercise they need. The rope seems to be spinning faster and faster and it's harder for you to keep up.

When you finally do stop, you're so beat up that you can't even think about cutting up an apple or snacking on a pile of grapes. So, what do you do? Grab a couple of doughnuts. No energy to make fresh fruit juice? No problem, just drink a cup of coffee to wake you up. Want to get out of the office for a couple of minutes? Stand outside the building, grab a cigarette, light up, inhale deeply, and forget about your troubles. The only problem is that, instead of giving you a break, these things are breaking you and you're making yourself much worse. Stress can increase your susceptibility to illness and suppress your immune system.

I see people in line at the grocery store or parents at my kids' soccer games who are worn out and stressed out. They need a break! It's really hard these days to make ends meet, take care of the family, and fulfill all your obligations. But you have to "jump out" sometimes. It doesn't have to be two weeks in the Caribbean—take a half-hour walk, spend a quiet day at home or a long weekend someplace nearby. Every day, I take the hour from 7 A.M. to 8 A.M., go to my office when it's nice and quiet, and think. It doesn't cost any money and it doesn't make me neglect my family or my patients. It just gives *me* back to me, so I can be there for the people in my life and the things I have to do.

Find out what your sanctuary is. It may be getting to the office an hour early to think, sitting on the dock with a fishing pole, practicing the piano, playing a round of golf, or just watching the world go by from your front porch. Relax, breathe, enjoy nature—whatever calms you down, schedule that into your everyday life. In the end, instead of taking up time, it will give you more time because you'll be refreshed and able to focus.

I know what some of you are saying as you read the Seven Habits of Healthy Living: I don't have time to do this. I'm too tired! Well, you'll have plenty of time when you're laid up in a hospital bed. Only you won't be able to do anything but lie there. By taking time to refresh yourself now, by taking a break from your usual routines to put the Seven Habits into practice, you are giving yourself time not just for today but for the rest of your life.

It's really hard these days to make ends meet, take care of the family, and fulfill all your obligations. But you have to "jump out" sometimes. It doesn't have to be two weeks in the Caribbean—take a half-hour walk, spend a quiet day at home or a long weekend someplace nearby.

My whole approach is about learning to Stop and Think and that doesn't take a lot of time out of your day or money out of your pocket. If you're too tired or too stressed out, you can't break old bad habits and you won't get clarity on what's best for you right now.

So, use the image of the kids jumping rope. Know that you've been jumping without stopping for too long. Jump out, take a breather, get yourself together, see what's important, reanalyze your life, and rest your body mentally and physically. Then, jump back in when you're ready. In fact, try it right now. Put the book down, get up and stretch, open a window, walk around the block, come back, close your eyes, and breathe deeply for a minute. When you're done, open up the book again. Ready to jump back in?

CHAPTER 10

Habit Number Seven:
Cleanse Your Body

N.Trani

WHY DO YOU NEED TO CLEANSE YOUR BODY? To clean the crap right out of you. And I'm not talking about undigested food. I'm talking about the real crap—pesticides, artificial flavors and colors, synthetics, chemicals in drugs, and toxins of all kinds that are not natural to the body. Here's one example we hear a lot about these days: mercury in fish. If you eat certain kinds of fish, trace amounts of mercury get into your body. The liver can't process it and there it sits, stored in your fat cells, building up until it causes real havoc. Get rid of it!

What does cleansing the body mean? Taking a shower? Washing

your hands? No, it means actually cleaning and resting the *inside* of the body. There are many cleanses available. It might still be a strange idea to you, but you will become more familiar with the different types of cleanses as they become more popular in the United States. And they are becoming more popular every day as people realize they've got to get the toxins out of their bodies.

The one type of cleanse that's probably the most familiar is fasting. Most religions advocate some kind of fast. When religious leaders developed these practices centuries ago, they were probably thinking of it in spiritual terms. But now we have science to support fasting for physical health as well. When you fast, you're cleansing by resting your body and giving it a chance to get rid of things that have been building up. But today we've gotten away from fasting. Instead, we take laxatives or some other kind of medication. That's not cleansing your body!

TYPES OF CLEANSES

There are a wide array of cleanses available, depending on your particular needs and desires:

- There are cleanses using herbs or nutrients that you take orally for cleansing the liver, colon, gallbladder, and the whole body.

- There are different types of fasts, such as water fasts and juice fasts.

- Even steady, rhythmic breathing is a form of cleansing: by exchanging gasses at a deep level, you are eliminating toxins.

- There are more invasive cleanses like a colonic or an enema, and some people prefer colon hydrotherapy, which was practiced much more in the 1800s and early 1900s. See a trained professional for this type of therapy.

- When you exercise and sweat, you are cleansing the body through your perspiration.

- Using a sauna is another good way to cleanse the body through sweating.

- Deep-tissue massage is also a form of cleansing. It's different from a light massage, and if you've never had one before, you might be surprised to find that within two or three days after the massage, you can become sick. It's actually a common occurrence. When they give you a deep-tissue massage, they're literally squeezing the toxins right out of you. Some people have told me they feel like they have the flu afterward and even begin to vomit after a few days. I explain to them that they were so toxic, the therapist squeezed so many toxins out of them, that they expelled the residuals by vomiting. If you have never had massage therapy at that level before, let the therapist know so the experience won't be too aggressive the first time. You can do it progressively to get the toxins out over time.

- For gallstones, there are different flushes and cleanses. If you decide to do one, I want to make it very clear that it should be done under the supervision of a health professional. If a gallstone is lodged in the common bile duct, you have a medical emergency that could be life threatening.

I am not going to tell you which specific cleanse to use, but I urge you to undertake the most intense forms of cleansing only with the guidance of a knowledgeable health professional. You need to talk to a professional who specializes in cleanses, someone who can evaluate your health and your concerns and advise what's best for you. Cleanses are powerful medicine! There is nothing like them to help you be healthy, but they can also be detrimental if you do not know what you're doing. You can hurt yourself. When you do cleanses, do them with the help of health professionals who know these cleanses well, know what to expect, and give you good advice for your particular circumstances. If you want to find someone in your area to go to, or an expert to consult with, you will have to do research. You can find out more or get referrals in your area from a local chiropractor, naturopath, or clinical nutritionist. You can even talk to the people running your local health food store to see if they can recommend sources for your search.

THE IMPORTANCE OF CLEANSING

How important is a cleanse? In today's world, it is more important than ever before. Why? There are more pollutants than ever before. Water isn't as clean as it used to be. Lots of chemicals are entering your body that you can't see, smell, or touch. No one knows all the things that

In today's world, cleansing is more important than ever before. There are more pollutants, water isn't as clean as it used to be, and no one knows all the things that are going into your body and how they are building up.

are going into your body and how they are building up. People in the health field generally consider that a dirty colon creates an unhealthy person. I agree. And I am very glad to see that colon cleansing is becoming a much more common option again.

When do you ever take the time to actually clean out the inside of your body? Do you do anything at all? Do not wait for the body to break down before you think about cleansing. For example, if you have to take medication for an illness or a disease, know that your medication is fixing one thing and compromising another. That being said, when do you decide to get the chemicals out of your body? A cleanse is the perfect opportunity to do that.

I have a lot of experience at a place called the Optimum Health Institute of San Diego, which also has a location in Austin, Texas. It's been around for nearly thirty years and I've been associated with it since 1991. It has a holistic mindset and looks at cleansing from the mind-body-spirit connection. It has the standards of cleanliness and knowledge that I require of a place where I would go for a cleansing experience. (For more information, visit www.optimumhealth.org) If you want to find an institute near you, ask family and friends who've had cleansing experiences, or consult with a natural healthcare practitioner for recommendations.

How often should you do a cleanse? It depends on your lifestyle and how you function. Do you eliminate properly—one major bowel movement a day? Do you eat fruits and vegetables, drink a lot of water, not smoke, not drink, not take drugs, and exercise? If you live your life in health care, cleansing once a year would probably be fine. If you live in disease care, as I've described it in this book, then you need to have more than one cleanse a year. Maybe two or three cleanses a year is better for you. Cleanses are followed for one week up to ninety days, depending on the type of cleanse.

Based on my experience, people who have gone through cleanses of the type and duration that's best for them experience a transformation. Everything comes to life: they think better, they function better, they have greater mental clarity, and they simply feel much better.

The seventh Habit of Healthy Living—cleansing your body—may be the one most unfamiliar to you, but make it part of your lifestyle. Take time each year to focus on cleansing your insides. You will be so glad you did.

CHAPTER 11

Bring the Whole Family Along

THIS IS A QUESTION I HEAR A LOT: "CAN YOU HELP ME WITH MY CHILDREN? How do I get them to eat more fruits and vegetables?" The problem is that lunchtime and snacking are gold mines for food manufacturers. Just check the shelves at the supermarket or watch the endless array of TV commercials aimed at kids—most products offer little more than a sweet taste and a lot of packaging. As a parent, you should be aware of the fruity, gummy concoctions marketed to youngsters. Check the nutrition facts and ingredients on the label. You will usually find little more than a sugar formula that only hints at real fruit. Pass it all by!

For snacking, fresh fruits are best. Dried fruits are the next best: they are sweet and have real nutrition in them. Dried blueberries have 10 grams of fiber in a half cup; figs and dates have 9 grams, apricots 8 grams, and prunes and raisins 7 grams. Figs are one of the richest sources of calcium outside of dairy products (144 milligrams of calcium in one serving). They're also a good source of iron, vitamin B_6, magnesium, and copper. One serving of dried apricots gives you one-fourth of the daily value of iron and enough beta-carotene for nearly three-quarters of the recommended dietary allowance (RDA) of vitamin A. So, why are you still buying those pricey chemical-filled, sugar-rich packaged items that have hardly any nutritional value and contain a lot of bad stuff?

There are other things besides dried fruits for healthy snacking. Try nuts, seeds, granola, pretzels, maybe even low-fat vegetable chips, but make sure to avoid treats made with partially hydrogenated vegetable oils.

Whatever you decide, get your children involved. Hold a tasting and let them tell you which healthy snacks they'd like to eat. And if they aren't getting enough good food because the meals in their school cafeteria are poor, or if they're always running to sports, lessons, friends' houses, and other activities and don't have time to eat right, then give them vitamin and mineral supplements, appropriate for their age. Our kids are really vulnerable to all the unhealthy trends in our society. We need to help them because they just don't have the knowledge and understanding yet to make good choices.

One of the best ways to lead your kids to better habits is by example. Share with them the news about healthier living. For instance, research shows a clear link between alcohol consumption and increased risk of breast cancer. If you're a woman, a wife, and a mother, what can you do? One, limit your alcoholic beverages. Two, keep your weight in check. Three, be physically active. And four, eat more vegetables. Tell your kids what you're doing and why—you are working to prevent breast cancer. And you want them to start preventing cancers and diseases of all kinds at a young age too. Show them how by doing it yourself! For men, one of the most feared cancers is prostate cancer. What can we do to help prevent prostate cancer? Eat a variety of vegetables daily, especially lycopene-rich, tomato-based foods. Maintain a healthy weight. Stay physically active.

These are actions that men and women can take. Your children will be men and women one day too. If they see you eating healthy food, snacking on fruits and nuts, exercising, quitting smoking, and learning to clear your mind and cleanse your body, your kids will start to do these things too. Start them early with these habits. By the time your kids reach the age when they're most at risk for developing diseases, these habits for staying healthy will already be second nature to them.

You may be sitting in a chair alone reading this book, but you don't live your life all alone. You share it with family and friends. Live the Seven Habits and show the people around you what it means to live in health care, not disease care. Bring them along with you. I'm not asking you to preach or to force. Have the bowls set up in your house filled with healthy foods, make an exercise plan and ask a friend to join you, cut out an interesting newspaper article about health and post it on the refrigerator. Show by example and the best example is how good you'll feel and how much energy you'll have.

> You can learn to stay healthy and make good choices every day. That's what the Seven Habits of Healthy Living are all about. When it comes to putting your body in a position to win, no one can do it better than you.

There isn't room in a single book to include every important fact and study. And there isn't room for every word of encouragement, every warning, or every wake-up call. I hope to continue the focus on health online: on my website—www.stopandthink.us—I'll update the health news with studies, reports, and information as it comes out.

You can learn to stay healthy and make good choices every day. That's what the Seven Habits of Healthy Living are all about. When it comes to putting your body in a position to win, no one can do it better than you. But sometimes we all need a little help to learn the facts and a little encouragement to keep going. And to stay on the road to health, we need to always remember: Stop and Think.

Notes

Chapter 1

1. American Institute for Cancer Research and the World Cancer Research Fund. *Food, Nutrition and the Prevention of Cancer: A Global Perspective* (Washington, D.C.: American Institute for Cancer Research, 1997).

2. S.M. Krebs-Smith, "Progress in Improving Diet to Reduce Cancer Risk," *Cancer* 83:7 (1998): 1425–1432.

3. E. Giovannucci, A. Ascherio, E.B. Rimm, et al., "Intake of Carotenoids and Retinol in Relation to Risk of Prostate Cancer," *Journal of the National Cancer Institute* 87:23 (1995): 1767–1776.

4. "52 Percent of Californians Are Overweight," *San Diego Union-Tribune* (June 14, 2000).

Chapter 4

1. U.S. Department of Health and Human Services, *The Surgeon General's Report on the Health Consequences of Smoking* (Washington, D.C.: U.S. Department of Health and Human Services, Centers for Disease Control and Prevention, National Center for Disease Prevention and Health Promotion, Office on Smoking and Health, 2004).

2. Ibid.

3. Lauran Neergaard, Associated Press, "Scientists Devise Formula for Predicting Lung-Cancer Risk," *San Diego Union-Tribune* (March 19, 2003), A7.

4. U.S. Department of Health and Human Services, *The Surgeon General's*

Report on the Health Consequences of Smoking (Washington, D.C.: U.S. Department of Health and Human Services, Centers for Disease Control and Prevention, National Center for Disease Prevention and Health Promotion, Office on Smoking and Health, 2004).

5. M.D. Johnson, N. Kenney, A. Stoica, et al., "Cadmium Mimics the in vivo Effects of Estrogen in the Uterus and Mammary Gland," *Nature Medicine* 9:8 (2003): 1081–1084.

6. U.S. Department of Health and Human Services, *The Surgeon General's Report on the Health Consequences of Smoking* (Washington, D.C.: U.S. Department of Health and Human Services, Centers for Disease Control and Prevention, National Center for Disease Prevention and Health Promotion, Office on Smoking and Health, 2004).

7. James P. Sweeney, Copley News Service, "Kids in Car? Then No Smoking, Bill Says." *San Diego Union-Tribune* (May 4, 2004), A1, A10.

8. Ibid.

9. Lauran Neergaard, Associated Press, "Scientists Devise Formula for Predicting Lung-Cancer Risk," *San Diego Union-Tribune* (March 19, 2003), A7. P.B. Bach, M.W. Kattan, M.D. Thornquist, et al., "Variations in Lung Cancer Risk Among Smokers," *Journal of the National Cancer Institute* 95:6 (2003): 470–478. The formula that can be used to calculate your own risk is posted on the website of the Memorial Sloan-Kettering Cancer Center: www.mskcc.org/mskcc/html/12463.cfm.

10. U.S. Department of Health and Human Services, *The Surgeon General's Report on the Health Consequences of Smoking* (Washington, D.C.: U.S. Department of Health and Human Services, Centers for Disease Control and Prevention, National Center for Disease Prevention and Health Promotion, Office on Smoking and Health, 2004).

Chapter 5

1. U.S. Department of Health and Human Services, *Alcohol and Public Health* (Washington, D.C.: U.S. Department of Health and Human Services, Centers for Disease Control and Prevention, National Center for Disease Prevention and Health Promotion, 2004); website: www.cdc.gov/alcohol/factsheets/general_information.htm.

2. Ibid.

3. Ibid.

4. National Highway Traffic Safety Administration (NHTSA), *Traffic Safety Facts 2002: Zero Tolerance Laws* (Washington, D.C.: NHTSA, 2003).

5. Ibid.

Chapter 6

1. G. Null, C. Dean, M. Feldman, et al., "Death by Medicine" (New York: Nutrition Institute of America, 2003).

2. Gardiner Harris, "At F.D.A., Strong Drug Ties and Less Monitoring," *The New York Times* (December 6, 2004).

3. Lauran Neergaard, Associated Press, "Scientists Advocate Stronger Warning Labels for Acetaminophen." *San Diego Union-Tribune.*

4. "Glaxo Chief: Our Drugs Do Not Work on Most Patients," *The Independent* (December 8, 2003).

5. Steven A. Brody, "The Menopause Question: Hormone Replacement Therapy May Not Be the Answer," *San Diego Union-Tribune* (March 18, 2004).

6. Gardiner Harris, "Antidepressants Raise Suicide Risk in Kids, FDA Says," *San Diego Union-Tribune* (September 14, 2004).

7. "Arthritis Drug Vioxx is Recalled: Health Risks Are Cited," *San Diego Union-Tribune* (October 1, 2004).

Chapter 7

1. John M. Jakicic, Ph.D., et al., "Effects of Intermittent Exercise and Use of Home Exercise Equipment on Adherence, Weight Loss, and Fitness in Overweight Women, a Randomized Trial," *Journal of the American Medical Association* (October 27, 1999), 1554.

2. The President's Council on Physical Fitness and Sports, 200 Independence Avenue, SW, Room 738-H, Washington, D.C. 20201; tel: 202-690-9000; website: www.fitness.gov. The Cooper Institute for Aerobic Research, 12330 Preston Road, Dallas, TX 75230; tel: 800-635-7050; website: www.cooperinst.org.

Chapter 8

1. "Overweight Americans Face Higher Cancer Risk, Study Finds," *San Diego Union-Tribune* (April 24, 2003).

2. John O. Holloszy and James R. Turk, presentation at the Experimental

Biology 2004 meeting, Washington, D.C. (April 19–23, 2004), *Proceedings of the National Academy of Sciences* (April 19, 2004).

3. *Tufts University Health & Nutrition Letter* (May 2003).

4. *San Diego Union-Tribune* (August 18, 2003).

5. Joint WHO/FAO Expert Consultation, *Diet, Nutrition, and the Prevention of Chronic Diseases* (Geneva: World Health Organization [WHO], 2003).

6. "Color Code Your Kitchen for Cancer Protection," *Environmental Nutrition* 24:6 (June 2001), 10.

7. "H_2O Health." *H_2O Chronicle* 1:1 (2003).

8. Ibid.

9. Ibid.

10. Ibid.

Index

Acetominophen, 54–55
Acid, 28
Acid-alkaline balance, 31
Actinidine, 87
Adrenaline, 38
Alcohol, 3, 6, 29, 35, 48–52, 104
  social problems with, 50
Alcoholics Anonymous, 52
Allicin, 78
Allopathic medicine. See Western medicine.
Alpha carotene, 78
American Cancer Society, 8, 65
American Heart Association, 8
American Institute for Cancer Research, 8
American Podiatric Medical Association, 62
Amylase, 34
Antacids, 26
Anthocyanins, 78
Antidepressants, 56
Antioxidants, 76, 84, 86
Appendix, 23–24
Ascorbic acid. See Vitamin C.
Asparagus, 85
Aspirin, 29
Attitude, 60, 91–95
Avocados, 85–86

Bacteria, 22
Berries, 86
Beta-carotene, 78
Beta-sitosterol, 86
Bile, 35–36
Blood glucose. See Blood sugar.
Blood sugar, 89
Body cleansing, 97–101
Body respect, 3–6, 11–18, 91–95, 97–101
Bone density, 44
Bowls of healthy snacks, 77, 89–90
Brain, 20, 33, 41, 49, 91–95
Brazil nuts, 86
Breathing, rhythmic, 98
Broccoli, 86
Brunner's glands, 37–38

Cadmium, 44
Calories, 61, 69–70
Cancer, 8–10, 65, 86, 89
  bladder, 44, 45
  breast, 9–10, 44, 50
  cervical, 44
  colon, 9–10, 38
  digestive tract, 10
  esophageal, 44, 50
  kidney, 10
  liver, 50

lung, 9, 44
mouth, 45
pancreatic, 44
prostate, 9, 50
rectal, 9
stomach, 9, 44
throat, 45
Carbohydrates, 73
Cardiac sphincter, 29
Cardiomyopathy, 32
Cardiovascular system, 40, 49
Cardiovascular workout, 63
Carotenoids, 76, 78, 78
Cataracts, 44
Chief cells, 30
Children, 56, 60, 103–105
   obesity and, 60
Chlorophyll, 89
Choices, 3
Cholesterol, 18, 35–36, 57, 86
   high-density (HDL), 35
   low-density (LDL), 35
Chymotrypsin, 34
Cigarette smoke. See Smoking.
Cleansing your body, 97–101, 105
   importance of, 99–101
Cobalamin. See Vitamin B$_{12}$.
Colds, 14
Colitis, ulcerative, 39
Colon, 38–40, 98, 99–101
Colonic cleansing, 98
Colon hydrotherapy, 98
Color in diet, 76, 78
Conventional medicine, 53–58
Copper, 87
Crypts of Lieberkuhn, 39

Deep Blue Supercomputer, 4–5
Detoxification, 34–35, 97–101
Diabetes, 14
Diabetes, type II, 72
Diet, 2, 8–10, 11–18, 47, 65–90,
   89–90, 98
   adding color to, 76–76, 78

changing, 74–76
high fat, 36
high fiber, 38–40
Standard American (SAD), 38
See also Food.
Digestive system, 19–41. See
   also Gastrointestinal tract.
Diverticulitis, 39
DNA, 89
Doctors, 46, 58
   questions to ask, 58
Drugs, 53–58
Drugs, prescription, 53
   safety and effectiveness,
   54–55
Duodenum, 37

Eating Well, 68
Enemas, 98
Environmental nutrition, 76
Environmental Protection Agency.
   See U.S. Environmental
   Protection Agency.
Enzymes, 89
   digestive, 23, 33, 38
Epinephrine. See Adrenaline.
Erectile dysfunction, 44
Esophageal ulcers, 28
Esophagus, 24–28
Exercise, 2–3, 6, 47, 59–64, 98,
   105
   recommended, 62–63
   starting a program, 61–62

Family health, 103–105
Fasting, 98–101
Fen-Phen, 55–56
Ferrari vs Volkwagen analogy,
   11–18
Fiber, 86, 88
Fish, 87
Flavonoids, 78
Folate. See Folic acid.
Folic acid, 85, 86, 87, 88

Food
  absorption, 36
  chewing, 21, 26
  ingredients, 66–67
  natural, 77, 81–83
  portions, 67–70
  shopping, 89
  super, 83–89
  See also Diet.
Free radicals, 84, 86
French fries, 68
Fruits, 6, 8–9, 13, 74, 76, 78,
   81–83, 103–105
  dried, 104
Fun, 2

Galbladder, 34–36
Gallstones, 36, 99
Gastroesophageal reflux disease.
  See GERD.
Gastrointestinal tract (GI), 20–41.
  See also Digestive system.
Georgetown University, 44
GERD, 28
GlaxoSmithKline, 55
Glucose. *See* Blood sugar.
Glutathione, 86
Green-yellow, 78
Gyri, 30

Habits, 43–101
Harvard School of Public Health,
   9
Harvard University, 9
Health, latest news on, 2
Health care, 3–5, 40–41, 105
Health longevity, 3
Heart disease, 44, 45
Heart attacks, 14, 29–30
Heartburn, 26–28, 29–32
Hepatitis C, 50
Herbs, 98
High-density lipoprotein (HDL).
  See Cholesterol.

Hormone replacement therapy.
  See HRT.
HRT, 56
Hydrochloric acid (HCL), 21
Hypothalmus gland, 20

IBM, 4–5
Immune system, 40, 45
Indigestion, 29–32
Indoles, 78, 86
Inflammation, 89
Information, importance of, 7–8,
   58, 89
Insulin, 33
Intestines,
  large, 38–40
  small, 34, 36–38
Intrinsic factor, 30
Iron, 88
Isothiocyanates, 86

Juice fasts, 98
Junk food, 3, 12–18
Justification of bad habits,
   15–18, 51–52

Kasparov, Garry, 4–5
Kiwifruit, 87

Large intestine. *See* Intestines,
   large.
Lentils, 88
Leukemia, 44
Lifestyle, 1–3, 11–18, 35
Limonoids, 78
Lipase, 34
Lipitor, 57
Liver, 34–36, 49
Longevity, 60
Low-density lipoprotein (LDL).
  See Cholesterol.
Lung disease, 44, 45
Lutein, 78, 87
Lycopene, 9, 76, 78, 88

Lymphatic system, 23–24, 37

Magnesium, 87
Massage, deep-tissue, 98–99
Mental illness, 61
Merck, 56
Microvilli, 37
Mind, cleansing your, 91–95, 105
Mouth, 21–23
Mucus, 30, 39
Muscles
    involuntary muscles, 25
    tone, 63
    voluntary-type, 24–25
Musculoskeletal system, 40

National Center for Chronic
    Disease Prevention and
    Health Promotion, 66
Nervous sytem, 20–21, 38, 49, 91
New York Times, 54
Nurses' Health Study, 9
Nutrition. See Diet.
Nutrition Institute of America, 53
Nutritional supplements. See
    Vitamins.
Nuts, 39

Obesity, 60, 66. See also Weight.
Omega-3 fatty acids, 87
One scenario, 15–18, 75–76
Oops scenario, 55–57
Optimum Health Institute, 100
Orange-yellow, 78
Oxyntic cells, 30, 37

Pancreas, 33–34, 38, 49
Parasympathetic response, 38
Parotid gland, 20, 23
Pepsin, 30
Pepsinogen, 30
Peptic ulcers, 44
Peristalsis, 27, 39
Pesticides, 83

pH, 30–31, 37
pH balance. See Acid-alkaline
    balance.
Pharmaceutical companies, 55–57
Pharmaceuticals. See Drugs,
    prescription.
Phytonadione. See Vitamin K.
Phytonutrients, 86
Pollution, 100–101
Portion size, 67–70
Potassium, 85, 87
Proteins, 88, 89
Prozac, 56
Ptyalin, 20, 23
Publications, recommended, 89
Pyloric valve, 30
Pyridoxine. See Vitamin B_6.

RDA. See Recommended Dietary
    Allowances.
Recommended Dietary
    Allowances, 90
Red, 76, 78
Red-purple, 78
Relaxation, 38, 41
Rope jumping, 93–95
Roses, Allen, 55
Rugae. See Gyri.
Running, 63

San Diego Union-Tribune, 45,
    65, 72
Sauna, 98
Seeds, 39
Selenium, 86
Self-healing, 3–4
Serotonin, 60
Seven Habits of Healthy Living,
    2, 10, 35, 40, 43–101
Shopping, 89
Small intestine. See Intestines,
    small.
Smoking, 3, 6, 43–47, 105
    quitting, 45–47

second-hand, 44–45
Snacks, healthy, 47, 77, 89–90, 103–105
Sodas, 72
Sodium bicarbonate, 38
Stationary bike, 63
Stomach, 28–33, 49
Stomach acid, 29
Stop and think, 1–10, 36, 46, 50, 57, 59, 60, 67, 79, 81, 86, 105
Stress, 93
Strokes, 9
Sublingual glands, 22
Submandibular glands, 22–23
Sugar, 70–73. See also Blood sugar.
Sulforaphane, 78, 86
Superfood, 83–89
Supplements, nutritional. See Vitamins.
Support groups, 46
Sweat, 98
Sweeteners, 70–73
Swimming, 63
Sympathetic response, 38

Teeth, 21–22
Tobacco. See Smoking.
Tomatoes, 88
Tonsils, 23–24
Toxins, 97–101
Trypsin, 34

Ulcers, 28, 38, 45
U.S. Centers for Disease Control and Prevention, 46, 60
U.S. Department of Agriculture, 72, 73

U.S. Food and Drug Administration, 54–56, 58, 73
U.S. Surgeon General, 44

Vegetables, 6, 8–9, 13, 74, 76, 78, 81–83, 103–105
Vioxx, 56–57, 58
Vitamin A, 89
Vitamin B complex, 85, 89
Vitamin B_6, 86
Vitamin B_{12}, 31–32
Vitamin C, 86, 87, 89
Vitamin E, 86, 87, 89
Vitamin K, 89
Vitamins, multi, with minerals, 90

Walking, 62–63
Washington University, 69
Water, 6, 28, 78–81
fasts, 98
Watermelon, 88
Weight, 9–10, 60. See also Obesity.
gain, 10, 47
Weight lifting, 63
Wellness, 5, 6–10
Western medicine, 43–58
Wheat grass, 88–89
White-green, 78
Wine, red, 50–51
Women's Health Initiative Study, 56
World Cancer Research Fund, 8
World Health Organization, 73, 83
Cancer Agency, 10

Zeaxanthin, 78
Zocor, 57
Zoloft, 56